Great LEGAL MARKETING

How Smart Lawyers Think, Behave and Market to Get More Clients, Make More Money, and Still Get Home in Time for Dinner

BENJAMIN W. GLASS, III

NEW YORK

Great LEGAL MARKETING
How Smart Lawyers Think, Behave and Market to Get More Clients, Make More Money, and Still Get Home in Time for Dinner

by BENJAMIN W. GLASS, III

ISBN 978-0-98371-250-3 Paperback
ISBN 978-0-98371-251-0 eBook
Library of Congress Control Number: 2011934412

Published by:
MORGAN JAMES PUBLISHING
The Entrepreneurial Publisher
5 Penn Plaza, 23rd Floor
New York City, New York 10001
(212) 655-5470 Office
(516) 908-4496 Fax
www.MorganJamesPublishing.com

Cover Design by:
Rachel Lopez
rachel@r2cdesign.com

Interior Design by:
Bonnie Bushman
bbushman@bresnan.net

FREE CD WITH AD EXAMPLES, TV AND RADIO COMMERCIALS

Would you like to receive a free CD with color copies of the examples I use in this book? Get periodic updates about the latest in lawyer marketing? Be among the first to know when I discover a new vendor or service that can help you get things done faster? Do you want the latest information on "Ethics in Legal Advertising" Notice (and my commentary)?

All you have to do is register your copy of this book.

Do it today and I'll also email you a copy of my free special report: *Why The Billable Hour is a Really Bad Business Model.*

Go to <u>www.RegisterTheBook.com</u>

FREE VIDEO MESSAGE AT LOSERFREEZONE.COM

Since the members of Great Legal Marketing are playing in a "Loser Free Zone" I've got a video message for you at LoserFreeZone.com. You might want to look at it now if you are near a computer because in the video I reveal the top three excuses that lawyers make for not being successful.

AN IMPORTANT NOTE FROM BEN GLASS

Hey, I'm A Lawyer. I've Got to Write A "Disclaimer," Right?

Besides, My Publisher Made Me Include This. Here it is:

This book is not intended to be either legal or ethical advice. While I am sure this book will inspire you, you should know that trying to copy one aspect of anyone's comprehensive marketing system without understanding "what is really going on under the hood" can be dangerous to your wallet.

Any copies of advertising used in this book are used solely for instructional and educational purposes. Any ad examples used are not to be ripped off verbatim by the reader. Certain marketing materials used in the marketing of BenGlassLaw may be licensed to my Great Legal Marketing Mastermind and Coaching members.

Legal requirements and ethical standards governing advertising, marketing, client relationships, communications, etc., for lawyers vary from state to state. They often seem to vary by whimsy. Only you are responsible for your own actions.

Neither the author nor the publisher makes any warranties, either express or implied, about whether any of the enclosed marketing documents, materials or instructions are legally or ethically appropriate in your jurisdiction. Neither the author nor the publisher accepts any responsibility or liability whatsoever for the legal or ethical appropriateness of any of the enclosed marketing documents, materials or instructions and/or your use of the same. If in doubt about the appropriateness of legality of any materials or instructions, you should obtain competent guidance just as you would with any marketing documents, materials or marketing plans you have developed or would develop on your own.

No income representations are made. Some lawyers learn the material in this book, take massive action and reap the financial, emotional and professional benefits that follow. Others will read this book, believe they have now "worked" on their marketing but won't follow through with anything. Whether or not a lawyer makes more money using this information depends entirely on the reader's proclivity to "take action," manage a law practice, and provide competent legal services. I and hundreds of lawyers across The United States and Canada are doing so, and I hope that you will join us.

ALSO BY BEN GLASS

The Truth About Lawyer Advertising
(TheTruthAboutLawyerAds.com),

Five Deadly Sins That Can Wreck Your Accident Case
(TheAccidentBook.com),

Why Most Malpractice Victims Never Recover a Dime
(TheMalpracticeBook.com)

Robbery Without a Gun (RobberyWithoutaGun.com)

**He has also co-authored numerous books for
entrepreneurs and business owners, including**:

*Shift Happens: America's Premier Experts Reveal Their
Biggest Secrets to Help You Thrive in the New Economy*

The Ultimate Success Secret (Ultimate-Success-Secret.com)

*Carry Your Own Leash: The Entrepreneur's Guide to
Autonomy and Success* (CarryYourOwnLeash.com).

**In addition to his books, Mr. Glass has also
created the highly sought after audio CD's:**

*Success in America: What Every American Should Know
About Leading a Life of Significance* (SuccessInAmericaNow.com)

Militant Time Management for Attorneys
(MilitantTimeManagement.com).

THANKS

I owe an enormous debt of gratitude to the folks who help make Great Legal Marketing possible. Tom Foster and Rem Jackson are my friends and business partners in the seminar side of my life. There would be no "GLM Conferences" without them.

Mairim Bartholomew, Mindy Weinstein, and Connie Gray help me produce more content than I ever thought possible. My sister, Terry Patterson, has managed the law office and protected my time for over 16 years.

Of course, nothing in my life would be as good as it is without my wife and best friend, Sandi, to whom I have been married since 1981.

Finally, I am deeply indebted to my friends Dan Kennedy and Bill Glazer for their advice to entrepreneurs of all types and for their personal inspiration to me to just "take action."

TABLE OF CONTENTS

PREFACE

The Difference Between the Average Lawyer and the Extraordinary Entrepreneur Running a Law Practice is Not As Great As You Might Think— You Only Need to Know That Others are Living an Extraordinary Life and That Their Success Can Be Discovered and Modeled.

My mission is to revolutionize the way lawyers market and build their practices, in order that they can have saner, more profitable businesses, live lives of significance and be heroes to their families.

I've designed this book to be both a "front to back" read as well as a resource guide for you to use for a particular marketing principle. I want to start by sharing a deep dark secret about marketing....

I can show you all of the whiz bang latest ads, search engine optimization techniques and social networking gadgets that are known to man.

They are all worthless.

They are all worthless IF you don't *get it* that the way you THINK about your law practice (a.k.a. "business") is far more important that any particular marketing technique or tool that you use. It's absolutely vital that you have an entrepreneurial mindset (or hire someone who does and then just do what they say) if you *really* want to make your law practice serve your family and your clients (in that order).

So....

You can go right ahead and *skip* all of the of *mindset stuff* in part one and just pick and choose random marketing techniques and tools to use....

You can go ahead and do it all right.... And then you'll be mad when they *don't work* for you...its' OK to be mad...but don't be mad at me. It is far more important (and may take longer to learn, frankly) that you begin to *think differently*. Remember your law professor saying that the first day of law school? Well, he was right in concept, but when he told you that *thinking like a lawyer* was the most important thing you'd ever learn for the benefit of your career, he was wrong.

Thinking *like a business owner* is more important. Guaranteed.

A NOTE ABOUT THE
GUEST CHAPTERS

There are many ways to be right about the complex and challenging problem of marketing your law practice in today's highly competitive environment. In fact a major way to lose the battle is to close your mind to anyone else's ideas. Another way is to simply keep doing the same thing over and over again, hoping for a different result.

Throughout this book you will find chapters or sections authored by my guests. You'll note that not all of the guests agree with each other on what is "best." They don't all agree with me! That's okay and I've deliberately left in the "differences." In the end it is up to you to develop a unique and comprehensive marketing campaign that fits your life, your practice and attracts your perfect client.

Many of my guest authors have developed some product or service that allows you to get to the next level faster. I know all of these authors personally and I do recommend their services.

However, once books get printed things can change. For the most up to date list of recommended vendors and services, visit GLM-Recommends.com.

CLOSE YOUR EYES AND IMAGINE THAT YOU ARE VIEWED AS THE MOST TRUSTED ATTORNEY IN YOUR TOWN

When you engage in a comprehensive, interesting and ethical marketing campaign you can become the guru through which all requests for legal information come. You can accept only those cases that fit your perfect case profile while making friends with both the declined client and the lawyer you refer them to. You can lock everyone up in "your herd" forever so that the next time they or anyone in their circle of friends needs an attorney like you, you will be "top of mind" (but you will not have spent millions of dollars in TV advertising to "brand" yourself.)

This is very achievable. Great Legal Marketing members across the United States and Canada are taking back the position of authority and trust in the community that lawyers once held. This book will start you on your journey.

Ben Glass

Part One

Forget the Fancy Marketing Techniques for Now

Get Your Head on Straight

About Why It is You Are Running a Law Firm in the First Place

Chapter 1

WARNING — SOME PEOPLE WON'T LIKE THIS BOOK

Heck, some people don't like me. This book is the product of years of being exposed to and learning "outside the box" marketing, and then using it to market my law practice. Several years ago I created the Ultimate Personal Injury Marketing and Practice Building Tool Kit, and Great Legal Marketing, LLC was born. I began Coaching and Mastermind groups, and today lawyers across the United States and Canada pay thousands of dollars a year to learn "Ben Glass style" marketing. Our marketing conferences consistently sell out even though we never offer any CLE "credit" for attendance.

I certainly have upset what I call the "marketing vultures" out there. The marketing vultures are all of the Yellow Pages reps, Mega Lawyer Directory website sales people, TV and radio advertising types, and the producers of junk "slap your name on top of this" newsletters whose answer for every failed marketing campaign is "you should have bought more." I've also upset the "professional marketing coaches" with their fancy alphabet soup letters after their names and their "certifications" from "coaching school" who call me and wonder who "certified" me to be a business and marketing coach. I often wonder: "Who certified their certifiers?"

As one, to remain anonymous, member of the Virginia State Bar hierarchy once said, "Lawyers either love Ben Glass or hate him." I teach lawyers how to differentiate themselves in their market place from the sleazy ambulance-chasing "your pain is my gain" types who are often no more than a marketing figurehead with scores of paralegals unethically settling cases. These folks are very upset, particularly with the publication of my book <u>The Truth About Lawyer Advertising</u> (TheTruthAboutLawyerAdvertising.com). I'm sure that I have also upset the "State Bar Advertising Committee-types" across the country who I have made fun of for their inane, time-wasting, business-busting view of commercial advertising and the First Amendment. Frankly, they've never seen the type of marketing that we are doing in the legal profession, and their thought process seems to be, "They never taught me this in law school, so there must be something fishy about it." This whole Internet thing has them really confounded!

Some lawyers do not like my "use your law practice as a tool to serve your lifestyle" attitude about running a law business. (Go to YouTube™ and search for "Is Ben Glass a Huckster?") As you read this book you will discover that my big idea is that your law practice should be used as a wealth-building tool. Now, before you close your mind and this book, understand that one key to being the best lawyer that you can for your clients is to build and nurture a profitable business that runs on systems and does not require you, the lawyer, to spend any time doing something that is not the highest value use of your time. It also requires that you understand that marketing is the most important job that you have in your practice. I don't care how good of a cross-examiner you are or that you take great depositions. None of that matters without a steady flow of new clients coming down through your automated and systematized marketing pipeline.

Finally, let me say that as you learn how to market your law practice and build a better business, you will probably shed some of your old friends. I have lost friends in the profession who still believe that "the law is a jealous mistress," and that 60-70-80 hour work weeks are and should be the norm. The good news is that my new friends-lawyers and other entrepreneurs who believe that each and every day is a tremendous gift and an opportunity to live life big and to live a life of significance, encourage me and inspire me to be better at all aspects of what I do. Popular motivational speaker Jim Rohn once said, "You are the average of the five people you hang out with most." I consider myself very lucky because I am hanging out with a bunch of lawyers who are energized each and every day about the practice of law.

I suggest that lawyers start thinking about marketing in an entirely different way. Shed the belief system that says that you must market to "all-comers," meet with everyone and accept every case that walks in the door. Get over the fear that if you start rejecting clients through complex marketing, you won't have any more clients. This has not been my experience nor the experience of hundreds of lawyers across the United States and Canada who have said "no" to traditional lawyer marketing.

Still interested? Or do you think this is too "outside the box?" Are you in the camp that believes lawyers shouldn't think about things like "profit", "value" or "running your law office like a business?"

You do have a choice. If you are perfectly satisfied with your life and your practice, then no need to read further. But if you believe that there is a better way to go about the business of the practice of law in order to lead the life you (and your family) want to lead, keep reading.

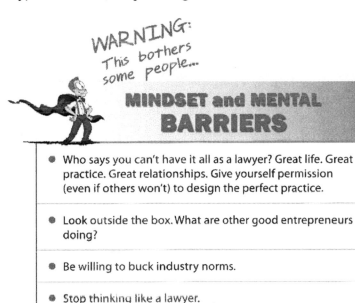

WARNING:
This bothers
some people...

MINDSET and MENTAL BARRIERS

- Who says you can't have it all as a lawyer? Great life. Great practice. Great relationships. Give yourself permission (even if others won't) to design the perfect practice.

- Look outside the box. What are other good entrepreneurs doing?

- Be willing to buck industry norms.

- Stop thinking like a lawyer.

Chapter 2

THE LAMEST EXCUSE FOR NOT LISTENING TO ME
"But Ben, *My* Practice Is Different."

The general reaction that most lawyers have when they first hear me speak or read one of my books or articles is that "Sure, that will work for you, but my business is different. You don't understand but my clients/community/business/ state ethics rules are different." Successful entrepreneurs adamantly reject this narrow minded thinking.

This belief is nothing but an excuse to stay inside your comfort zone. The marketing and mindset ideas that you are holding in your hand are working across the country and in Canada. They work in other professional practices and in other businesses. The reason they work is that people are people. We are all wired pretty much the same way and no matter whether we are selling a widget, a car, an idea or a service, consumers make decisions about what they will buy and whom they will work with pretty much the same way.

I know, I know. This concept is almost heresy in the law business. "We are different." "Ours is a 'calling' not a commodity." I heard that too for the first two decades of my career and all I can tell you is you have a choice. You can keep on using that type of thinking as a way to limit your growth and you can keep on doing what you've been doing if you're entirely satisfied with your life and your practice.

Or

You can make a change. Successful entrepreneurs recognize that doing what you've always done and thinking that this time, you are going to get a better result, is nuts.

It's Just Really Dumb to Think That Just Because
You are a Lawyer Things are *Different*

Chapter 3

FIVE REASONS WHY LAWYER MARKETING IS <u>SO</u> HARD

I told you earlier that the mindset part of lawyer marketing is the most important aspect of your practice. Before we go there, however, I want to remind you of the enormity of the task. Anyone who tells you that lawyer marketing is easy or can be done "one step" or that they have the "magic blue pill" has never run a small law firm. Firms of five lawyers or less probably have it the hardest. They face enormous competition caused in part by the collapse of "BIGLAW" in the last few years and in part by the continuous pumping out of brand-new lawyers by the law school factories. In both cases, other lawyers are discovering that the only way they may end up making money is by opening up their own practice. To make matters worse, in any major metropolitan area there are firms willing to spend millions and millions of dollars on lawyer advertising to compete with you. Yes, it is harder than ever to differentiate yourself in this very saturated marketplace.

I can help.

Most lawyers that I run into are very frustrated with their marketing. They tend to spend a lot of money randomly copying exactly what other lawyers have done, but they really can't tell you whether they've made money or lost money on any particular marketing campaign. They buy marketing and advertising out of paranoia that if their ads stopped running, they would never see another case. Trouble is, most of what they learned about marketing came from watching what other lawyers were doing, As a result one lawyer's ad tends to look pretty much like the next lawyer's ad.

Frustrating:

Here are the top five frustrations that lawyers have with marketing their practices:

Reason #1: People ignore lawyer advertising

Heck, people ignore all advertising. We couldn't survive if our brains did not deliberately tune out most of the 5,000 marketing messages we are exposed to each day. Yes, that's right. Up to 5,000 messages a day. When I first heard that number, I thought that it was grossly exaggerated. Then I spent a few days looking for and at all of the marketing messages that each one of us face every day. From the side of the coffee cup that you are drinking out of in the morning, to the logo on your laptop computer, to the ads in the newspapers and magazines that you look at daily, and even to the inserts in all the bills you get at your home and office, you are being shouted at by marketers.

Your brain would go into overload and shut down if it tried to actually listen to and understand every single marketing message it encounters. Think about it. If you don't actually have a squirrel running around in your attic, you paid no attention to the pest control ad that was blaring on the radio as you drove into the office today. Need a mortgage? If not, you ignore those little charts in the real estate section of your local newspaper that showed this week's mortgage rates buried amidst the mindless and copycat marketing done by most residential real estate agents.

Your advertising is no different. You push messages out into the market using TV, radio, Internet, and Yellow Pages, marketing to millions of people, yet on any given day there is only a very small subset of the population who actually:

1. Need a lawyer in their lives, and
2. Haven't already gone out and hired one.

The rest of the people are ignoring you and even if they "heard" your ad today they probably won't remember it next week when they <u>do</u> need you.

On the other hand, think about the last time you bought a car. You likely did not suddenly get the idea one day and make a decision the next. You followed a process. Somewhere along that process, you started to think about maybe getting rid of that old clunker and getting yourself something new. That thought grew in your head and you started to "research" cars on the Internet or talked to your friends about their cars. As your thinking about a new car moves along, you probably began to pay attention to one or two particular brands or models. What happened next? You began to "see" these particular cars every day on the road. You began to hear ads and perhaps saw articles in the papers about these particular cars that you were looking for. Guess what? These cars had always been on the road and these ads had always been running. Your brain just ignored them until you actually started to become interested in a particular brand or model. Your subconscious did not even allow these advertising and marketing messages "in" until you were looking for that information.

If the car marketing was any good at all, it felt like it was designed just for you. It answered your questions as if it was designed to "enter the conversation already running through your head." At some point you indicated to the car dealer that you were interested. Your being "affected" by the car dealer's marketing was a process.

Today, one of the keys to really effective lawyer marketing is to figure out how you can make your marketing interesting enough that even people who are not in need of a lawyer today will pay attention to you. Will talk about you. Will keep you top of mind so that whenever they or anyone in their circle of 50 (everyone knows 50 people who would come to their funeral) need a lawyer in your specialty, they think of you. Traditionally, lawyers have attempted to achieve this type of top-of-mind presence through spending millions of dollars running ads or trying to develop something cute, such as talking frogs, fistfuls of cash, or offering you the impossible-"quick claims-no office visit-cases settled in 30 days." They rely on "name recognition and recall" marketing. This type of marketing gets attention all right, but it is not the attention that most of us are seeking.

Reason #2: There's a ton of competition out there.

The second reason that lawyer marketing is so hard is that everywhere you look there's a lawyer. Think about it. Open up the Yellow Pages Directory in your neighborhood. The likelihood is that there are still 70 to 100 pages of lawyer ads even today when (almost) no one uses the Yellow Pages to find *anything*. Go ahead, type YOUR SPECIALTY, YOUR CITY AND STATE into Google and see what is returned. For any legal specialty in any city, there's lots of lawyer web pages showing up on Google. Hundreds or thousands of them in some cases. Lawyers are all over the television and in "specialty directories" at the end of grocery store check-out counters. They pop up on park benches, billboards and the sides of busses. Moreover, there's no doubt that unethical lawyers are still using in person solicitation in hospital emergency rooms or doctor's offices as a "marketing tool."

You have a lot of competition. According to the American Bar Association, there are over 1 million attorneys in the country. Heck, InfoUSA.com, the largest list broker there is for mailing addresses, has a database of over 300,000 personal injury attorneys alone. No matter where you are located the consumer is faced with a ton of choices for legal services. And, since the consumer is generally a poor judge of the quality of legal services it doesn't matter a wit if you are the best attorney in town. In fact, being the best attorney around is generally *no marketing advantage at all.*

Reason #3: Our image.

The third reason that lawyer advertising is so difficult is that, particularly for personal injury attorneys, we have largely shot ourselves in the foot with our efforts to grab the attention of the consumer.

Carton Bank ©*The New Yorker Collection 1989 Danny Shanahan from cartoonbank.com. All rights reserved*

"Your pain is my gain" type advertising makes injury attorneys an easy target for the insurance industry and other tort reform advocates. Ask people on the street about lawyer advertising and you will probably get a generally negative reaction. Tell someone at a party that you are a "personal injury attorney" and see how quickly they disengage. (Interestingly, those people in need of a lawyer right now tend to have a different, more positive view of lawyer advertising.)

Can you really blame people for thinking badly about lawyers? It's hard to expect the public to think highly of you when you have attorneys like Stephen Conrad, a former Woodbridge, Virginia attorney, who pled guilty on August 19, 2008 to federal fraud charges in connection with a scheme to defraud his clients. According to court documents, Conrad, who primarily represented personal injury and worker's compensation clients, settled clients' claims without their authority or knowledge by forging their signatures on release of liability forms and then submitting those forms to the insurance companies against whom the claims were made. He then forged their names on the checks and helped himself to the money. He did this to the tune of $3.7 million dollars. (Courts then turned their backs on Conrad's former clients who tried to undue the settlements-another black eye for the profession.)

Who can forget Jim "The Hammer" Shapiro, the New York "tough, smart," personal injury attorney who's commercials promised to "hunt down" defendants and "wring everything" out of them. Problem was that when Shapiro was sued for under-settling a case, a New York jury awarded almost $2 million to his former client. At trial the jury Shapiro admitted that he had NEVER tried a case in court.

And it's not just personal injury lawyers who are embarrassing the profession. Have you heard of Jackson, Michigan lawyer Richard McQuillan? This guy was sentenced in 2009 to six to 10 years in prison for stealing close to $1 million from the estate of a now deceased client.

And then you have Nashville, Tennessee lawyer David Weed, who was appointed in 2001 to recover stolen state money intended to benefit poor children. He was indicted in Memphis on charges that he stole funds. Weed was made overseer of the assets of Cherokee Child and Family Services, an agency that had a contract with the state to place Memphis children in subsidized child care, and then Weed allegedly stole more than $100,000 from accounts he controlled! In April 2010 Weed, admitting that "there is no question I am guilty," pleaded guilty to several crimes. Unbelievable.

Here's the good news. When you apply the principles taught in this book, your marketing efforts become not only more effective and less costly, but they position you as "not like those other lawyers." (Oops, I did it again. See? I just now upset a whole bunch of lawyers who think that I should not be mentioning "a few bad apples" or suggesting that your marketing can be used to lead a consumer to quickly eliminate any lawyer using "old style" marketing. Too bad.)

I've had people whose cases I did not accept tell me that "Ben, you are not like those other lawyers they talk about." When I inquire further, the potential clients have told me that "they" are the "greedy lawyers who sue everybody and who are driving up the cost of medical care and killing our economy."

The other good news is that by using the principles I teach, you not only raise your own image but you improve the image of all lawyers. By providing good, useful, and helpful consumer information to people as a major part of your marketing efforts, you start on the path of letting people know that lawyers are good people. Look, I know that you probably have been doing this for years with your talks to your clients and potential clients in your office. You probably have been educating people about the tort system, about insurance companies, and about why it is important that the United States legal system be both respected and protected. You know about the power of a jury and you've been teaching it. What "Ben Glass style marketing" does is help you take that message to the masses. Take it to all of the people (including those in your community who will be your jury in the future) who are attracted by your marketing and who come down through your marketing funnel. Individually, we'll never compete with the millions and millions of dollars spent by the insurance industry to pollute the minds of the public, but each one of us can do our part and fight back against the efforts of the tort reformers to misinform the American public.

Reason # 4: The ethical rules hold us back-or do they?

A fourth reason why lawyer marketing is so difficult is that we believe that the ethical rules that regulate our advertising constrain us. To some extent, that belief is well founded. The knuckleheads involved with some of the state bar advertising committees either have never had to run a real business on their own, or have never looked at the First Amendment and the cases interpreting it and "commercial speech" or both.

It is amazing to me how some lawyers have so much time and creativity to come up with ways to try to tell other lawyers how NOT to market. Here are some examples:

1. New York's recent effort to ban "pop-up" advertising on YOUR website. Come on now! A ban on a particular Internet technology in a medium (the Internet) in which technology changes dramatically every six months?

2. The Florida State Bar's ban on certain <u>sounds</u> in lawyer advertising. Can you imagine this? Advertising committee members in Florida with nothing better to do, huddled in their room, listening to the audio of radio and TV ads. The sound of bouncing balls is out, and the sound of giggling children is in. Or is it the other way around? How can a sound be deceptive? Doesn't matter to the Florida State Bar, apparently. Sounds

are a cool thing to regulate. Besides, they'd all have to find productive jobs if they weren't looking busy reviewing all those ads.

3. Some states want to charge lawyers a "legal advertising review fee" whenever you post a new video on YouTube—even if the video is not "advertising!" Lawyers are just now discovering the vast uses for video technology on the web. Here's what I would do if I practiced in a state where I had to submit every video: I'd make a big long one… about eight hours long…and submit it. At least that way you'd get your money's worth.

4. How about the Kentucky State Bar's position that each and every one of your monthly office newsletters must be submitted and pre-approved 30 days before you mail it? What if the New York Times had to go through censorship pre-approval each morning before it hit the streets? Lawyers should be mailing their clients 12 to 24 times a year. (Snail mail. With stamps. Delivered by mailmen. Not email.) Newsletters should be current and topical. Done correctly, there's actually very little "advertising" that need be done in a newsletter. The Kentucky State Bar's newsletter approval process is a blatant infringement of the First Amendment. Moreover, it acts as an additional, unwarranted, tax on the practice of law because there's a fee associated with every review. But guess what? The 30-day pre-approval process does not apply to blogs. What's the rational basis for that distinction?

5. How about that North Carolina State Bar? It challenged the advertising of an attorney who stated that he was a member of the "Million Dollar Advocates' Forum." Their committee met and issued a letter and here was their beef: Since the "Million Dollar Advocates' Forum" is limited to trial lawyers who have demonstrated skill experience and excellence in advocacy by achieving a trial verdict, award or settlement in excess of $1,000,000.00 or more, the ad in question which indicated that membership was limited to those attorneys who have settled cases in excess of $1,000,000.00 was *misleading*. The North Carolina State Bar also took the time to point out that the ad misstated that the membership was limited to those who had settled cases in excess of $1,000,000.00 where **the truth** was that those who had achieved verdicts or settlements in the amount of exactly $1,000,000.00 were also included. The Bar felt that this was apparently grossly misleading to the public. Misleading enough to spend valuable time in meetings acting "busy" in the over-regulation of lawyer advertising.

6. How about the Connecticut State Bar advertising committee? They do "website audits." They believe that running advertising that says "Attorney Glass limits his practice to [any particular specialty area]" is somehow misleading.

What? You cannot tell the public that you don't practice in 49 areas of law, and that you limit your practice to 3 areas of law? The Connecticut State Bar is in effect compelling the lawyer to waste his most precious asset, his time, by now having to handle the calls and inquiries from potential clients who have legal matters he does not handle and does not want to handle. This requirement is nothing less than a government-mandated theft of time. Don't these people have anything better to do?

Yes, it seems that the advertising committees of the various states are out to get lawyers. "Ben Glass style" marketing, done well, allows the consumer to recognize you as the wise man or woman at the top of the mountain without you ever having to come close to any ethical line.

Keep reading and I'll prove it to you. (By the way, Great Legal Marketing members get timely information and analysis of lawyer advertising ethics rulings and opinions. Months later, when most lawyers are finally recognizing the additional restrictions their state has just enacted, our members have already implemented the "solution.")

Reason # 5: Lawyers and law firms-difficult to differentiate

The fifth reason why lawyer marketing is so difficult is that the public can't tell a good lawyer from a bad lawyer. This is true not only with lawyers, but any professional service business. Think about it. Before you go to a doctor, do you really know whether the doctor is any good or not? Ask any medical malpractice lawyer whether they see "repeat offenders" in their medical community. Of course they do. Why would a grossly bad doctor have any patients at all? The answer is that the public has no easy way to judge the quality of professional services.

Even the designations such as "Super Lawyers™" and "Best Lawyers in America™" aren't all that helpful. Look around. Lots of people have those designations. These organizations publish books and magazines that…are you ready?…make all of the lawyers in the books and magazines look the **same**! Remember, the more lawyers designated as spectacular the more plaques they sell! Now that they have spawned all sorts of competitors the public is right back where we started: not being able to tell a good lawyer from a bad one. (By the way, that was an absolutely brilliant idea to create the whole "Super Lawyers/ Best Lawyers" thing. Have you seen the prices they charge to advertise in those magazines? Lawyers will pay a lot of money to have their egos stroked. Yes, I'm in there too-but I'm not buying any advertising space from them. It was a brilliant idea, however.) Fortunately for you, 99% of all lawyers in those "Best of" directories have no clue about how to leverage their fame.

● ●

Ben's Bonus Success Tip #1

What To Do if You Are Designated "Super"

As soon as you get your designation you begin receiving all sorts of offers to buy plaques, reprints and website "badges." Just take the letter they send you "congratulating" you on your designation frame it and hang it up in your office. It has the same effect and it is free!

● ●

So, yes, it's great if you are the best lawyer in town. Great, for your current clients that is. It is <u>NOT</u> a marketing advantage. How many "really good" lawyers do you know who remain broke because they believe that 'if you work hard and try significant cases, clients will beat your door down?" How many still preach this myth to young lawyers? some of you will put this book down right now because of that last sentence. Oh well. The rest of you can keep reading.

Why is Lawyer Marketing
SO HARD?

- Through an effective multi-million dollar campaign, the insurance industry has *poisoned the well* against America's lawyers, and lawyers have contributed to that message with DUMB ADVERTISING.

- 99.0000% of all people were not in an accident yesterday so *there is no reason to listen* to most lawyers'"messages"

- Competition—over *90 pages of lawyer ads* in the Yellow Pages in many major metropolitan areas.

- 3,000 - 5,000 marketing messages a day—media is getting cheaper, so expect *more noise*.

- The internet is *so vast!* (websites, blogs, videos, social media, articles, online directories, etc.)

- They forgot the *marketing and business-building class* in law school!

- Recession threw *lawyers out of big firms* and into a town near you.

- Never-ending *choice of media*—where do you begin?

- Good marketing is *complex.*

- We are already SO *busy!*

- Marketing *vultures.*

- Ethics-*restrictive.*

Chapter 4
GET A LIFE

Ask any of your lawyer friends whether they feel they can "have it all" as an attorney and "have it all" in the rest of the aspects of their lives and they will probably look at you with crossed eyes. To most attorneys these two concepts appear mutually exclusive. The summer before my oldest son headed off to law school, the school sent him a number of books about "the law school process" and "life as a lawyer". Sadly, these books portrayed life as a lawyer in a very unbalanced, "sacrificial" way. At his graduation from law school retired Supreme Court Justice Sandra Day O'Conner spoke in part about their futures, including a future with a "new master," the client. I think she was wrong. You had better not let your client be your "master."

I can remember, as a young lawyer, being told by other "wise and experienced" attorneys that the "law is a jealous mistress" and the fact that I was spending more time in airports than I was at home was just "all part of the practice of law." I bought their lies hook, line and sinker, as I am sure did most of the people who were graduating with my son.

Looking back on those early years as a lawyer, I can now see that their view of the world and of the profession was like a poison that I allowed to seep into my mind. Their belief system about the law had become my reality. At that time, whenever my wife and family complained about my being on the road, they were the ones who were wrong, because "you don't understand, this is the way it is supposed to be." It is no wonder that lawyers have come to "expect" the reality that the life of the law is a life unto itself.

For some that reality never goes away. During my legal career, I have represented partners at some of the largest law firms in the country—people making millions of dollars a year. While "wealthy" (or at least earning a lot of money) they often expressed their frustration at still having to "grind it out" in order to continually justify to their partners their share of the money pot. While their responsibilities may have changed since the time they were young associates, their workload and giant trades they were making for "success" had not.

• •

Ben's Bonus Success Tip #2

Giant Trades Lawyer Make for "Success"

Time – *Stolen from family. While the clients' work always gets done.*

Health – *Stolen from self. You may be shortening your life by years.*

Family – *What are they going to remember? What have you missed already?*

Sanity – *Stolen by easy access to you via cell phone and email. If you can't think of a better way to value yourself than to make yourself available 24/7, then you need to work on your positioning.*

I am not willing to trade away any of these. You don't have to either. All you need is to build a business that works for you.

• •

Fortunately for me (and now for you because you are reading this book), I figured out that they were wrong. Looking back, I admit that it took much longer than it should have, but I will defend myself by saying that when all I was are surrounded with—when all I read—when all that comes from the podiums of the seminars I attended taught that the life of a lawyer is supposed to be a grind, "that's just the way it is," it's hard to see the bright blue sky. It took me many years to give myself permission to both search for a better way and to then embrace it.

My belief system started to change when, after 12 years of working for someone else, I left my old firm and started my own solo law practice in Fairfax, Virginia in 1995. As those of you who have started your own firm or business know, the birth of a new enterprise is daunting. By sheer force of all the things that need to be done in getting that business off of the ground, you are compelled to think about other things besides the legal aspects of your life. You are forced to learn new things, read new materials and to figure out how to balance it all.

At first the sound of your keys opening the lock on the front door of your own law firm sounds terrific. Freedom at last. But freedom from what?

Those first few years were a real struggle. Burdened by the old way of thinking about things and not knowing anything about marketing a practice other than what I had seen other lawyers do or what I had been taught by the folks selling the marketing (a.k.a. "the marketing vultures"), I forked over tens of thousands of dollars to buy exactly the same crap they were selling to every other attorney in town.

In those early years of running my own practice, where for the first time I was the one responsible for getting the clients, I was puzzled. Here I was with a ton of good education and a bunch of experience and a pretty good track record of achieving success for my clients, yet the marketplace didn't seem to acknowledge my success by rewarding me with more clients. Prospective clients should have been able to see the obvious—I was a good lawyer and they should come to me. It bothered me greatly to see lawyers who I knew didn't actually know their way around a courtroom running big "double-truck" Yellow Pages advertising and getting clients from it. Didn't these prospective clients know that the insurance companies laughed at these attorneys and their "we never go to trial, but we can sure churn a bunch of cases" attitude?

Something else bothered me. I knew business owners and entrepreneurs in other industries. They weren't lawyers—they ran bagel stores, car repair shops and home renovation companies. Most not only had no graduate education, but some never went to college. Their businesses were thriving. Some were making a lot more money than I was. How is that fair? Isn't the rule that the more formal education you get the better off you'll be once you're in the working world?

Then one day my life changed. Someone recommended that I read Napoleon Hill's book <u>Think and Grow Rich</u>. It was a book that I'd actually seen many times at the bookstore. I didn't know who Hill was and had never bought the book because it seemed a little slimy and misleading—how morally ethical is it to just "think—and grow rich?"

I bought <u>Think and Grow Rich</u> and read it. Then I read more about Napoleon Hill and how that book had come to be. It seems that Andrew Carnegie had offered Hill, a young journalist, the opportunity to go on a mission. Carnegie wanted to know if there was a "secret to success" and thought that a good way of researching the problem would be to have Hill interview the brightest entrepreneurial and business minds of the time to see whether there were commonalities in the way these men (yes only men at the time) thought and behaved. If patterns of thought and behavior could be ascertained then perhaps one could know why some people end up more successful then others.

Hill's discovery of 17 principles of success, which he first wrote about in a major treatise and then distilled in <u>Think and Grow Rich</u> got me thinking. What if I looked at successful business people and entrepreneurs outside of the lawyer industry to see if I could find patterns of thought and behavior that made them successful and could be modeled to change my law practice? Was that possible?

Around the time that I was discovering Think and Grow Rich I was also fortunate to hear from some lawyers at major conferences who were talking about "balance." Shockingly, they talked about not accepting every case and about not believing that a lawyer had to be everything for everyone. Indeed, both clients and potential clients were not to be "masters" over you. You are the legal consultant and advisor. You tell them what to do—not the other way around. You control how they communicate with you—not sleep with your cell phone next to your bed. That message resounded with me and I started to explore it further.

These lawyers talking about balance exposed me to scary numbers and statistics about lawyers for whom the burden of the practice of law have become so great that the profession destroyed not only their businesses but in some cases their families and themselves. Back in 1990 a Johns Hopkins study looked at 104 occupations to see which professions suffered from the highest rates of depression. When adjusted for socioeconomic factors, lawyers, no surprise, topped the list and were found to suffer from clinical depression at a rate of almost four times that of the norm. Can you imagine if that same study was conducted after the recent economic tsunami?

So I made a choice and slowly I began to change the way I thought about the practice of law and its relationship to the rest of my life. I challenged assumptions. I challenged "authority." I challenged industry norms. I challenged myself to change.

What I discovered was that there really are no rules. There certainly are no rules that say that a lawyer cannot have a life and be a lawyer. Moreover, not only can one be a great lawyer and have a great life, but I discovered that having a great life and a balanced existence leads to being a better lawyer. Think about it yourself for a moment. Are you a better lawyer and problem solver when you've got piles and piles of files on your desk and the phone rings off the hook incessantly by anyone who's got a question for you or is it when you sneak away with one file to your quiet place away from your office where you really do your best work? Do you feel like an air traffic controller at the end of the day having spent 8 or 10 or 12 hours just trying to keep the clients from hitting each other or are your days filled with the balance of health, fitness, relationships, sanity and satisfaction of having really gotten something done in moving a client's problems toward resolution?

I made a remarkable discovery: you can create, first in your mind and then in your actions and behaviors, a well balanced life and lifestyle outside of the law. Then, rather than the business of the practice of law imposing itself on your lifestyle, you can do it the other way around and have your lifestyle imposed on your business. It's okay. I promise you that if you will simply give yourself permission to think this way your life your practice will improve. You will, of course, meet a wall of resistance. The "Eeyores" of the profession will tell you that not only is this not possible, but it is not "right." Let them go. There is a reason they are Eeyores.

Go Ahead-Have a Life!

Ben's Bonus Success Tip #3

By the way, if you haven't already listened to it, get the audio CD of my talk to students at Christopher Newport University, "How to Be Successful in America," (SuccessInAmericaNow.com). After you listen to it, get some copies for your kids.

Chapter 5

THE WAY REALLY SUCCESSFUL ENTREPRENEURS THINK AND BEHAVE

Running the attorney coaching and mastermind groups at Great Legal Marketing, the local Glazer-Kennedy Insider's Circle™ (Glazer-Kennedy-Virginia.com) mastermind groups in Northern Virginia and participating in several other high-level mastermind groups with entrepreneurs and business owners from across the country has given me a unique perspective on what it is that successful business owners have in common. For the most part it is not where they were born or where they grew up or went to school. Many do not have college degrees and only a few attended the "very best" colleges, universities and law schools. In speaking with many of them and getting "inside" their businesses I see patterns of thought and behavior that many have in common.

The good news is that you don't need to have been born "this way" to be a successful attorney entrepreneur. Everything I know, and from what I can tell, everything that the most successful attorneys who I work with know, came from learning along the way.

There are two ways to learn something new. You can learn by trying something, making a mistake and then making a correction. This approach works but can be long and painful. Smart entrepreneurs use a second method. They look around to see what other successful people are doing and they adopt the good ideas and implement them into their businesses. They leverage other people's experiences. As you will see, later, hanging out with people smarter than you is a really good idea.

In June 2009, I was marketing and advertising guru Dan Kennedy's[1] guest on the Glazer-Kennedy monthly Diamond Coaching Call.

On that call we talked about effective marketing for professional practices and covered a lot of different strategies. Throughout the conversation, however, we kept coming back to the mindset side of the equation and at the end of the hour Dan Kennedy said:

> You know, what we are talking about is that there really are two different types of people in the world: The first, when he sees an idea will say, 'I can't do that,' or 'That won't work in my business,' or 'They'll never let me do that.' The other type of person, when introduced to a new idea or strategy that has been successful in another business or niche, says, 'You know, I may not understand everything that I just heard, but I do know that there may be a very valuable key there and if I can figure out how to use what I just heard in my practice/business it may be a real goldmine for me.'

• •

Ben's Bonus Success Tip #4

Really successful people, when exposed to something new, say:

"You know, I may not understand everything that I just heard, but I do know that there may be a very valuable key there and if I can figure out how to use what I just heard in my practice/business it may be a real goldmine for me."

• •

Take a good look at yourself. What type of a person are you?

You can be exposed to all of the great marketing and advertising ideas that have been passed down over the years and never really "get it" unless, at the same time, you think and behave like an entrepreneur. You need not have started and built several other businesses to run a successful law practice but it certainly does help to see yourself not just as a lawyer, but as a business owner and visionary. In *E-Myth*, Michael Gerber describes the business owner as wearing three hats:

- The technician—the one who can successfully carry out those skills unique to being a lawyer—usually at an above average level;

---

1   Dan Kennedy and his partner Bill Glazer, have made a profound impact on my life. I'm not kidding. You should be getting their "No B.S. Marketing" newsletter. It's the one newsletter that I read, cover to cover, the day I get it.. Try it free, plus attend their really cool webinars and get an "Income Explosion" guide. Check out **DanKennedyAndBenGlass.com.**

- The manager—the person who oversees, deals with and solves the day-to-day running of the business;
- The entrepreneur—the visionary, the one who looks into the future and says: "what's next?"

As you go through this book, then, you need not be prepared to enact every strategy you see or even to understand fully what is being discussed. I'm asking now only that you open your mind to what it is that other very successful, very ethical lawyers who are leading balanced lives and doing great jobs for their clients are doing. This is much more about how you behave and think than it is about how big your Yellow Pages ad is.

Here are the ways successful entrepreneurs think and behave:

Success Principle 1—The Number One Predictor of Success is Who You Hang Out With

Who do you hang out with? We call this "the power of association." Look around. Do you associate with people who do things bigger, better, faster and bolder than you do or do you associate with whiners and losers? The best way to learn how to make five times more than you do now is to hang out with people who are making five times more than you do now. They know something that you don't. They know something that the losers and whiners don't. <u>All</u> of the successful entrepreneurs that I know are part of at least one "mastermind alliance."

In *The Law of Success,* Napoleon Hill defined the mastermind as:

"A mind that is developed through the harmonious co-operation of two or more people who ally themselves for the purpose of accomplishing any given task." In *Think and Grow Rich* he makes this analogy: "A group of brains coordinated (or connected) in a spirit of harmony, will provide more thought energy than a single brain, just as group of batteries will provide more energy than a single battery."

You may need new friends. That's okay. You'll have a lot to choose from.

• •

Ben's Bonus Success Tip #5

Don't take Eeyore to lunch. Hang out with people who are positive about the profession, about life and about themselves. Stay away from those who spend their days blaming others for their woes.

• •

Success Principle 2—Profit is Good

We are neither shy nor embarrassed about making a profit for the work we do and about attempting to extract as much profit out of our businesses as we can. Yes, most of us did go to law school because of that altruistic gene that we have that says, "Help people." The undeniable truth is, you can't help people if you're not making money. If you are worried about whether the lights are going to turn on Monday, whether you're going to have competent staff there, whether you can pay the bills, whether you'll ever get a new call from the next client, you cannot help somebody and you cannot be the best that you can.

Let me ask you this question: Do you have more stress or less stress when the dollars are down? Is your advocacy, brief writing and counseling you give to clients better or worse when you are not burdened by the fear and worry that comes with a cash flow crunch? In order to be the very best you can for your clients, your family and yourself you have to be making a profit with your law practice. The lawyer who is running a business that includes a marketing machine that drives potential clients to him in order that he can select out and represent only those clients who best fit his skill set, attitude and interests is a better lawyer for those clients. Don't worry if you can't save everyone. You were not put on this earth nor are you expected to save everyone. That's impossible. It leads to mediocrity and burnout. Your role is to take your unique gifts and talents and maximize those for the people you can help.

So, when they say, "Oh, well that Ben Glass, he's just a marketing lawyer." That's okay. I'm running a business that's making a profit that's good for my family, putting my kids through school and helping me be a really good lawyer to "A" clients. What's wrong with that? I guarantee that if you bring up the subject of "extracting maximum profit" at your next local bar association meeting that they will whisper about you in the halls.

Ignore them.

Success Principle 3—Greed is Good—Be Very Greedy With Your Time

I call it militant time management. Go ahead- be a jerk with your time. We put locks around our doors and windows, we put our money in the bank to keep it safe, and we buy expensive software to "protect our identity." Why then, are we so willing to let people stick their hand into our wallets and steal our time, our only irreplaceable asset? You must know and appreciate the value of your time and the value that you give to the world.

One retired judge recently told me: "The reason that so many 50—60 year-old attorneys are on their second or third marriages is that they took on this 'jealous mistress' when they were younger, bought into the lie that 'this is just the way it is so tough it out' and totally ignored the person they had once fallen madly in love with."

Here are 5 Time Management Keys that I adhere to. I expound upon them in my "Militant Time Management for Lawyers" program (www.MilitantTimeManagement.com).

1. Relate everything you do to your goals.
2. Calculate the true value of your time and delegate everything else that is not at your "pay level."
3. Do not make or take phone calls that are not scheduled in advance.
4. Throw out your typical "to do" list. You are going about things the wrong way.
5. Educate your employees and clients as to why your time is so valuable and why it is in everyone's best interest to protect your time.

Success Principle 4—Successful entrepreneurs have an abundance mentality.

There are lawyers who have actually written me to complain that they are "disappointed" that I am teaching, on a national basis, something that I had been sharing on a private basis to a limited number of people for years because now "everyone will know the secrets and everyone will be doing the same thing."

That's dumb.

First of all, everybody is pretty much doing the same thing right now and have been ever since lawyers started advertising. All you have to do is look in your local Yellow Pages directory or at most attorney websites. Second, these lawyers think way too much of themselves if they believe that all of the millions of people in their community are paying attention to all of their marketing and flocking to their doorsteps. Obviously, that's not true.

In my attorney marketing mastermind group, (lawyers who pay up to $18,000.00 a year to meet in person three times a year to discuss marketing and practice building) I have several lawyers who are in Virginia, including two who are in my community and who practice in the same area of law as I do. On the one hand I could have a "I've got a secret and I won't share it with you" attitude about what I teach. I recognized early on that inviting people who were smarter than me into my group and hanging out with them was a good idea for my life and that there are far more cases and clients out there than any one lawyer or law firm could possibly handle. A rising tide lifts all boats. So what if all of the attorneys who compete directly with me on a local basis end up making more money for themselves and improving their lives? I'd much rather be one of them than an outsider!

Great entrepreneurs believe that the world is big and that the opportunities are endless. When you truly believe this, your entire thinking about the ideas that you see changes. What I have found is that lawyers who are exposed to those ideas, but tend to stay mired in mediocrity in their practices and their lives do so because they have a scarcity mentality. They live their lives looking over their shoulders, because they believe there is not enough of everything to go around. Thus, they not only refuse to share what it is they know, but they refuse to open their minds to the possibilities. I pity them.

Success Principle 5—You, Not Allstate Are Responsible For Your Financial Security

It is so easy to assign blame for your own lack of success to *the other*. For years I've listened to lawyers blame insurance companies, judges, other lawyers, clients and the economy for their own lack of success. Really successful entrepreneurs don't make excuses. They accept the reality, for example, that the CEO of an insurance company owes a duty to his stockholders, not the lawyer's accident client, to maximize profit. That is his moral duty. It is your responsibility to figure out how to get what your client deserves.

It's just way too easy to join in that "group whine" of despair. Run away from it when you hear it. All you have to know is that no matter where you are in America, there are lawyers who are highly successful and doing well in any economy/jurisdiction/practice area. Successful entrepreneurs in other businesses know that around every Wal-Mart, there's a mom and pop hardware store that is thriving. The smart business owner takes responsibility for his own welfare, seeks out the "winners" and says: "What can you teach me about how you have achieved and maintained success?" Being a winner is much more about the choices you make than it is about what others do.

Success Principle 6—Challenge Industry Norms (a.k.a.: "Who Made THAT Rule?)

If you went into an occupation or a profession and you had no mentor and you didn't know what to do to be successful, Earl Nightingale said the best thing you can do is look around, see what everybody else is doing and just do the opposite. I told you earlier that you want to model what the successful people are doing. However, if you don't know who the successful people are, or can't find any, then simply look around at what the rest are doing and do something different. Doing what everyone else is doing is the sure path to "average." By definition, what the masses are doing is merely average. That should not be good enough for you.

For example, if you were going to run an ad in the Yellow Pages, the very first thing you would do is look in the Yellow Pages and see what all the other ads look like. You would immediately notice that all of the other ads already look like each other. How smart is it to copy what's already there and just insert your name? I don't care how many pages you can afford to buy or whether you can get the front and the back cover; you'd be an idiot to run exactly the same ad as everyone else is running. Yet this is exactly what the marketing vultures are selling you. You would be engaging in what my friend, Richmond, Virginia DUI Attorney Bob Battle (BobBattleLaw.com) calls "random-chance" marketing. (Gee, "I just hope they choose my firm by some random chance because my ad looks no different from anyone else's ad.")

Some of the "industry norms" in the legal profession are:

1. The best way to get your name out there and get cases is to join a whole bunch of committees, so that you can get referred everyone else's "dog" cases.
2. In a plaintiff's practice you have to not only risk all of your time, but also totally fund all of the cases yourself.
3. In order to satisfy and keep clients, you have to make yourself available 24/7 and give them your cell phone number.
4. A case isn't done until you have deposed and interrogated every witness.
5. In order for your TV or radio ad to be effective people must hear it at least seven times.
6. It is a mistake to not keep renewing that Yellow Page ad.
7. My type of clients won't respond to "that type" of marketing.
8. White space on an ad "sells."
9. No one will read "all of that information" in a copy-dense print ad.
10. If I don't sign up the client today they will go to the next lawyer on the list tomorrow.

Reject them.

Success Principle 7—It's OK to Practice Discrimination

There is a perfect client profile for your practice and skill set and you should be marketing only to that person.

Who do you enjoy representing? What type of client brings you not only the money that you deserve, but also the enormously good feeling of helping someone solve their legal problem? Which type of client do you hate? Are there "dog cases" right now sitting in your file cabinet or on your computer? Successful entrepreneurs give themselves permission to recognize that there is a perfect client for them; to design that prototype in their minds and commit it to paper; and then to design marketing and build a practice that is specifically for that type of "A client."

It is okay to treat the potential client you want differently than the clients you don't want. In fact, your marketing should repel those whom you do not enjoy representing.

Go ahead. Discriminate.

Success Principle 8—Recognize That We Are Not in the Commodity Business.

I once heard a personal injury lawyer at a marketing seminar say that there was no way he could differentiate himself from his competition. "After all," he said, "we are the same."

If you believe that just put this book down and go back to what you were doing yesterday. I'm here to tell you that it's absolutely not true.

If you believe that all you are doing is producing the same widget that every other lawyer in your niche is producing, then you are doomed to a no better than average career. I hope that you do not believe that you and your practice are a fungible commodity, yet this mentality is exactly what most lawyers "say" with their marketing.

Here are some ways lawyers can differentiate themselves:

1. Develop a unique selling proposition. They dig deep to answer this question (first posed to me by Dan Kennedy): *"Why should I choose you to do business with, above all other choices, including the choice to do nothing?"*
2. They niche their business. They don't try to be all things to all people.
3. They create and sell an experience. Think "Starbucks."

4. They create, sell, and deliver by a system. Think "McDonalds."
5. They create an interesting and educational system to market their practice that is so deep and comprehensive that people come to know you by your type of marketing. At my firm, BenGlassLaw, the entire marketing effort is centered on <u>a unique first message:</u>

If you have been, Involved in an Accident you Might not Need an Attorney,

But before you:
Talk to the Insurance Adjuster
Hire an Attorney
Or Sign Any Forms
Get Our Free Books

Here is one of our print ads with our unique message. This ad was approved by the Virginia State Bar after a ridiculous tussle over the font size of the words "Legally We can't say" and " …no one can." The ad appears on a magazine that is in virtually every doctor's office and hospital waiting room in our area and is, behind our websites and newsletter, the third most powerful tool in our marketing arsenal. This is followed by a marketing system that delivers an information package to them automatically and repeatedly. Your marketing system clearly delivers two important messages:

1. A description of exactly the type of case we are looking for.
   and
2. Step by step instructions on "How to Shop for and Hire a Lawyer.

Success Principle 9—Immunity to Criticism

Here's a guarantee. When you start to celebretize yourself and run ads that teach consumers how to "read lawyer ads" you will draw fire from your competition. There are many who believe that the <u>only</u> way to attract clients is to "do well and they will come." Others will be upset that you have exposed their misleading advertising. They will talk about you in the halls and behind your back.

Let them have their fun. There are few who are actually qualified to judge you or your advertising. Remember, the only person who is responsible for your ultimate success (or lack thereof) is you. They aren't paying your bills for you. As long as your advertising is ethically sound you should simply ignore the voices of the critics who say "well, who gave you the 'right' to write a book?"

You Know Your Marketing is Effective When They Sling Arrows!

Chapter 6

SUCCESS LEAVES FOOTPRINTS

By: Rem Jackson, Top Practices *(TopPractices.com)*[2]

"Success Leaves Footprints" —Dan Kennedy

If I've learned anything in the last few years it's that I'm not as smart as I once thought I was. I was a successful executive working for a very big company and I ran a multi-million dollar division. I had a lot of people working for me.

I was organized and I was effective.

I really was. I had learned how to work through others and had become a very accomplished manager and leader. When there was a problem, I knew exactly what to do, and even better, my leadership team that I had trained extensively knew exactly what to do. I had it all figured out.

Then I left the big company and started my own small company.

Oops. When something broke or something went wrong, I couldn't just watch as my team swung into action. I couldn't bask in the glory of my colleagues marveling at my team and how good they truly were. I actually had to (gulp) fix it myself. At least at first I did. And while I had to do that, I had to write the

---

2   Note from Ben: Rem Jackson is my personal mindset coach. He is one of the few people in the world who actually does have my cell phone number because he has helped me innumerable times "get back to center" when the whole world seems to be shaking at once. Each month Rem and I host a "mindset" coaching call for my Mastermind and Coaching members. This is one of the most popular programs at Great Legal Marketing.

, answer sales calls, help clients, do the budget, the books, clean
pers on the floor, go to the post office....

Turns out, I wasn't so organized and effective as I thought I was. Not
even close.

It's at this point where most small business owners, most doctors, lawyers,
professionals of all kinds start to crack. Some make it through, but they are
usually scarred with the wounds caused by long hours, stressful days and nights,
frustration and fear. Most don't even make it, they "go back" to what they know-
working for someone else.

That didn't happen to me. I think partly because I am a smart experienced
professional who drew on every possible resource I had. But the real reason I
survived this entrepreneurial crisis and later thrived was because I was willing
to learn from others.

I accidentally fell into exactly the right place I needed to be. I accidentally
did what I am suggesting you do quite intentionally. I found out that successful
people do things pretty much the same. They really do-all of them (at least the
ones I know). I also found out that they are quite willing to leave footprints and
let you walk in them. In fact, if they hold their secrets tightly and don't leave
footprints. Following them is a complete waste of time anyway.

I lead the Top Practice Marketing Mastermind Group. This is a group of like-
minded individuals (mostly doctors) who are willing to share their best marketing
and practice management ideas and strategies with each other. I learned how to
do this by hanging out with many of the people who you'll be hearing from in
this book. Jim Rohn famously said, "You are the average of the five people you
hang out with the most." Scary thought for a lot of us. If you pay attention to the
television or follow the news obsessively closely, you become convinced that we
are all doomed and things are getting worse every day. There is no opportunity.
Resources are scarce and finite. But not in my world. I live in a world filled with
abundance and my life is enriched by helping others as they help me.

It's just an easier way to live. Rich and abundant.

As you prepare to learn what Ben and his guest authors are ready to teach
you, let me tell you what they all have in common.

First, they know where they are headed. Their course is plotted and they
are working their plans. They have what Napoleon Hill called "Definiteness of
Purpose." I call it goals. ONE OF THE BIGGEST SECRETS IN LIFE IS THAT
YOU MUST WRITE DOWN YOUR GOALS. You can't keep them locked in
your head. They need to be on 3 x 5 cards and in pencil so you can change them

regularly. If you don't do this, then you are merely wishing for things. You must have your goals written down and you must review them regularly. I do it twice a month when I change my contact lens.

You Can Download Rem's Goal Worksheets at RemsGoalWorksheets.com

Second, they associate with smart, positive, people who can teach them what they know. Napoleon Hill called this Masterminding. Winners love to hang out with other winners. We can't stand listening to the whining lists of "why things are especially hard for me" that keep most of us drugged. You need to spend time with people who can reset your brain. People who can recalibrate your ideas. People who think so big that you can't help but see how possible something is that moments ago you thought impossible. Bring yourself into alignment with smart positive people you trust and you will find out that their success really does leave footprints and you will move quickly towards attaining your goals.

Finally, they bombard their brains with positive influences through reading and listening to recordings. Winners are voracious and curious. They have to get the latest book. They are constantly buying and consuming positive, useful information. And they begin to increase the pace at which they learn. They turn off the TV and stop doing useless mindless things on their computer and they hit the reset button on their brains. As they do this, they begin to inoculate themselves from negative thoughts, and fears. They see fear the way that Glazer-Kennedy's Bill Glazer has defined it as False Events Appearing Real.

Success leaves footprints. It truly does. Develop the habit of learning something new every day. Look for it. Don't stop until you find it. Read. Mastermind. Associate with other winners, and write down your goals so that you can focus like a laser on what you truly want your life to be. What your definition of success is. I've adopted this definition-"Living Life on My Terms." I believe that says it all. As I've learned and grown and associated with others like Ben Glass and Tom Foster, I've come to see something that surprised when I looked behind me…I saw that I was leaving …footprints.

About the Author:

Rem Jackson is the President and CEO of Top Practices, LLC, and the leader of the Top Practices Master Mind Group. Top Practices is a company dedicated to helping professionals and businesses reach their professional and personal goals by building their "perfect practice". He can be reached at rem@TopPractices.com. You can find out more about Top Practices at www.TopPractices.com

Part Two

The Building Blocks of
Lawyer Marketing Success

**While Specific Tools and Techniques Change Over Time,
the Principles of Great Legal Marketing are Timeless**

Chapter 7
THE BIG PICTURE

Let me give you a 30,000 foot overview here. As you consider your options as to how to spend your next hour or your next dollar on marketing your practice, revisit this chapter often.

Here is your model:

1. Recognize and accept that good, effective marketing is complex. There is no "easy button."
2. <u>You</u> (and only you) decide who you want to see coming through that door as your next client.
3. You need to have a good database that will automate the marketing for you.
4. Grow and cultivate your "herd" of raving fans.
5. Communicate with your raving fan base 12-26 times per year, mostly utilizing an interesting, <u>mailed</u> (not emailed) newsletter.
6. Perfect your "inbound media." They are looking for you on the internet and (to some extent, in some places), the yellow pages.
7. Be found by understanding and maximizing your website's search engine optimization.
8. Attract attention and create interest with headlines and compelling copy that "enters the conversation running through the prospects mind."
9. Make an irresistible offer that compels the prospect to raise their hand and say "please tell me more!"

10. Deliver information products that convince your "perfect client" that you are the wise man/woman at the top of the mountain.
11. Be relentless in your follow-up.
12. Continue to grow and cultivate the herd.

"Ben Glass Style" MARKETING 101

- Shout a different message.

- Give them a really good reason to initiate that first contact with you.

- Make them an irresistible offer that gets them to not only contact you first, but stop their search while they are waiting for you to respond.

- Their request for information is followed by your sequential mailing and e-mailing of responses.

- Be bold! Tell them what cases you are looking for.

- You want to "be everywhere," so when they start to research you, they determine that you are a major center of influence.

Chapter 8

GOOD LAWYER MARKETING IS COMPLEX

Lawyers sometimes visit me at my office to *pick my brain* about marketing. Typically, I'll bring them in and show them <u>all</u> of the things I do to get a client. I'll take out a blank sheet of paper and draw the flow chart of all the things that occur to get a client to raise their hand and say "I'm interested" and then all of the things that happen to them once they do. I'll show them the steps I <u>force</u> clients to take before they can meet with me.

Most leave disappointed. They were looking for the magic bullet—the ONE thing they could do to get more clients. The easy thing. The tweak in their Yellow Pages ad that would make the phone ring or the quick tips for Internet marketing that would help them dominate Google in their market area. They can't believe that I don't meet with every client who wants a free consultation and that my marketing material deliberately dissuades certain clients from even calling for an appointment.

Getting clients is a complex problem. As I noted in Chapter 3, there is a ton of competition in your market niche; consumers don't know how to tell a good lawyer apart from bad; ethical rules appear designed to make all lawyer marketing look the same; and your marketing messages competes with 3,000-5,000 other marketing messages a day.

Most lawyers look for the simple solution to this complex problem. They add color to their Yellow Pages ad, buy "double truck" right next to the six other lawyers who use that "solution" and they let web designers create the prettiest websites that brag about the law firm and its years of "combined experience" but end up looking like everyone else's website.

There are no simple solutions for complex problems. There are only complex solutions for complex problems. *That's good news.*

A multi-step, multi-media marketing system that is complex can serve to:

1. Differentiate you from the lawyers who rely on the old two-step marketing approach that consists of buying and ad and offering a free consultation;
2. Establish you as the wise man/woman at the top of the mountain without you having to say so;
3. Ward off those "C" and "D" clients that you hate by forcing them to *qualify* for your representation;
4. Increase the transaction value to you of each client, thus *reducing* your case load in order to allow more time for family and other things you *really* like doing while you make more money.

Here are the *objections* I hear about implementing and using a complex, multi-step, multi-media marketing system:

1. If I don't personally contact the client right away they will go to another lawyer because your system is too slow.
2. My clients don't want to read all that stuff.
3. I need to do the little cases for the chance to get the big case later on.
4. The little cases don't take up that much time and they pay the rent.
5. You do all that for each client? That's too expensive.

Here are my responses:

The *I Must Deliver an Immediate Personal Response* Syndrome

Do you really want to be viewed in your community as a commodity? Are you really so plain and fungible that if they don't hire you as their lawyer the next lawyer will do just as well? People who are just looking for coffee pull into whichever gas station or fast food restaurant appears next on the road. People looking for an experience *plan* their route to Starbucks. Which do you think is the better buyer? Which is the better customer?

If the fear is that *I may miss the big case if I don't make myself available 24/7* then I've got news for you. You are missing cases already. You don't get all of the cases in your town right now, do you?

Consider this: if you needed non-emergent heart surgery would you rather go to the doctor who can't see you for six weeks or the one who says, *come on in, I'm not busy, let's do the operation today!* Which do you *perceive* to be a better doctor?

By the way, our own data reveals that clients in serious personal injury cases are taking anywhere from four to twelve months after they enter our marketing funnel to sign a contract with us. What we found is that no other attorneys are marketing to them during these months. It is a huge mistake to believe that if you do not sign a client on the first phone call, he or she is hiring someone else. It's not true.

● ●

Ben's Bonus Success Tip #6

Earl Nightingale said: *"With anything in life, if you don't have a mentor, you don't know whom to ask, you don't have a group to talk to, at least look around and see what everybody else is doing and recognize the only way to get out of that box of being average is to do something different and to avoid copying what everyone else is doing."*

● ●

But, Ben, They Won't Read All That Stuff You Send Them

Those that won't are the same ones who won't take your settlement advice later. The truth is that they may not want to read all of your educational material, but since no other lawyer is sending them a big package the very fact that you are doing so makes you unique. This lawyer must know what he's doing, look at all the good quality educational stuff he is sending.

Of course, the reason we include the DVD and the audio CD in addition to written material is precisely because some people will learn by reading, others by listening, and still others by watching. The DVD is shot like a TV interview and it even includes commercials (for your law firm, of course.) The commercials reinforce the message that the smartest thing they could ever do is to ask any other lawyer they are interviewing for his big package of information before making the decision as to who to hire. Guess what that other lawyers' answer will be!

Preparing all of this educational material gives you a good reason to keep sending the potential client information. We drip our initial mailings out over 14 days, reinforcing our message. The potential client may be talking to other lawyers, but every few days he or she is getting another package or email from us. Time and time again we have been told by potential clients who hired us that it was the follow-up that caused them to decide to hire us. They tell us that even if they interviewed other lawyers all they got was a "thank you" letter or a slick brochure that was all about the lawyer (and not the problems the client was having.)

Finally, sending multiple packages of information gives you a reason to call potential clients, in a helpful way to ask whether they have received your information, read it or watched it on their TV and do they have any questions? Low key. Non-pushy. Your materials sell you without you having to sell you.

If I Don't Do the Little Case for Them Then They Won't Call Me for the Larger Case Later

This objection relies upon a false premise. The premise is that if you do a good job for them in the little case they will remember you later. Try this test. Start asking your clients who have had other cases who represented them in the past. They won't be able to remember. They can't even tell you the name of the surgeon who operated on them five years ago. Merely doing a good job does not make you memorable enough to get a future referral.

The key to rejecting small value cases or cases with dubious liability is to do so in a way that both sets you up as the *big case lawyer* and offers a good reason as to why you can't accept every case. One reason for not accepting every small case is that you have many big cases to work on. Those cases take time. Another reason is to talk about how you spend your non-work hours. That's right! Explain to them that you don't work nights and weekends, because you are with your family, on ball fields or at dance recitals. This will make you memorable.

The key is that no matter whether you accept or reject a case, you stay in front of that prospect *forever* with an interesting *monthly* newsletter. If you carefully explain why you don't take small cases and stay in front of the prospects monthly then they will remember you when they or someone in their circle of influence needs a *big case* lawyer the next time.

The Little Cases Aren't That Much of a Hassle and Besides, They Pay the Rent

Really? Have you ever actually tracked the time you and your staff spend on the little cases? Let me ask you this: if you have an hour to spend don't you think it's better spent increasing the value of a $100,000 case by 10% than it is to increase the value of a$10,000 by 10%. You don't have unlimited time, do you?

Though I don't have statistics to prove it, my experience is that the clients with smaller cases also tend to be the same ones who don't listen, don't take advice and use an inordinate amount of your office's time. Far better to develop a referral or of-counsel relationship with a younger, less-experienced lawyer whom you can mentor as *they* work on the smaller cases.

A Complex Marketing System Must Be Expensive

It could be. But I often hear that objection from lawyers who are spending money year after year in the Yellow Pages, running ads that sit right next to their competitors and say the same thing as their competitors. Thy build giant brochure websites that don't get traffic and don't convert the traffic they get.

It's very hard to market without spending any money, so the issue becomes *how will I spend my next marketing dollar?*

The BIGGEST MISTAKES
You Are Making With
Your Marketing   Part 1

- Failure to *study the competition* to see what message they are using so that you can *send a different message*—or worse, just copying what they do and relying on the "random chance" the consumer will call you and not your competition.

- Failure to *automate the marketing* so that new leads are accumulated and communicated with while you sleep or play.

- Failure to realize that the hightest and best use of your time is to learn to *create and execute effective marketing*.

- Failure to maximize the *power of the Internet*—lots of websites, blogs, videos, etc.

- Failure to recognize the value of and *capture every name and address* you can.

- Accepting the *"you should just buy more"* strategy.

- Failure to use *massive follow-up* marketing campaign.

- Failure to *hang out with very effective marketers.*

- Failure to *market as a specialist.*

- Not using an effective *call-to-action.*

- No *book* written.

Chapter 9

YOUR MOST IMPORTANT ASSET—YOUR LIST

The most important asset of a law firm is not the fixtures, the computers or even the people. The most important asset is "the list." It is that collection of names and addresses of everyone who has ever expressed any interest in hearing anything you have to say. These are people who will give you permission to market to them.

The list is made up this way:

1. Every person who raises his or her hand to request any of your information
2. Every potential client who comes from any other source, but who has contacted you
3. Local attorneys who do not compete in your area of expertise
4. All of your vendors
5. All of your local friends and relatives
6. Other professionals who would likely be in a position of influence to people who see them as the wise man/woman at the top of THEIR mountain.

You need a software database that:

1. Automatically adds everyone who fills out a contact form at your website into your list.
2. Can easily import contact information from your existing client management software.

...ell you what specific marketing piece the prospect saw to drive them to you.

4. Can be easily used by your staff to add new names and contact information when the initial contact to your office is by phone.
5. Can automatically respond to each new prospect inquiry in a way that is personal to that inquiry.
6. Can easily segregate and "slice and dice" the names so that your top referral sources can be easily identified and marketed to differently and different segments of your list (i.e. clients vs. vendors vs. other lawyers) can be marketed to differently.

For years my database of choice has been a program called InfusionSoft. It is online software that manages my entire law practice and two additional businesses. It allows me to not only easily gather contact information, but to create multistep multimedia follow-up marketing campaigns to anyone who enters our final. It literally runs my life!

I have set up a video and an online demonstration for you at **GLM-Software. com.** If your current database software doesn't actually market while you sleep" then you need to look at this video.

Chapter 10

DECIDE WHO YOU ARE GOING TO MARKET TO

Do you have problem clients? Are there people you represent that you and/or your staff hate? Do you sometimes ask yourself " Why the heck did I take this case?"

Here's the problem <u>and</u> the answer: **You.**

- You didn't have a clear vision of your perfect client.
- You didn't clearly communicate to your staff what your vision is.
- You believed, mistakenly, that you must serve everyone.
- You feared that you would never get another client.

I'd like to give you <u>permission</u> to start believing today that you have the right to market to <u>your</u> perfect client. The potential client you don't like may be perfect for someone else (maybe a competitor!) but as long as we are talking about *your* law practice I want *you* to market to the client *you* want.

You don't need to represent everyone.

Yes, there are lots of other (good) cases out there for you.

Sit down today and describe your perfect client /case. Write the description down. Now, create marketing that *talks directly* to that person.

Hint: If you or your firm have multiple practice areas then you should have multiple, distinct, *perfect client* profiles. Do not try to shortcut and create marketing pieces that try to speak to everyone at the same time! You ad will be watered down if you try to make the ad do too much work! Yes, you must create different ads for different practice areas. Remember, good marketing is complex.

So, if a major problem in your practice is crappy clients, then remember:

- Your marketing attracted them
- Your fear of never having another client "made" you accept them
- The same fear prevents you from "firing" them right now

Who are you REALLY Marketing to?

- Other owners of herds—referral-based marketing. Everyone knows 50 people who would show up for their funeral!

- Those not currently in need of an attorney—growing the "herd" of those who find you interesting.

- Those currently in need of an attorney—they are looking for someone like you right now.

Marketing Can Solve That Problem

Chapter 11

TALKING TO YOUR FANS WITH A NEWSLETTER

Most lawyers prefer to skip over the chapter about newsletters and skip to something sexier like the internet or TV. Getting an interesting, mailed newsletter out the door each month is <u>work.</u> It's much easier to write a check to the TV ad rep or design one yellow page ad that you won't need to change for 12-15 months.

The truth is that it costs at least 8 times as much to obtain a new client as it does to have an old client return or refer. Done properly, a newsletter not only tells the world who you are and what you stand for but it enables others to repeat your story to their friends.

Here are some tips for getting your newsletter out the door monthly:

1. First, don't do it if all you're going to do is slap your name on someone else's 100% canned newsletter. I've seen these newsletters and they are drop-dead boring. Lawyers send them to me. They go straight into the trash can. If your newsletter reads like the latest brief to an appeals court you are better off sending your postage money to charity. The "canned" newsletter providers know nothing about how to market a law firm.

2. Keep a folder by your desk into which you can place interesting ideas that come across your desk or enter your life through the month. It is terribly difficult to start writing a newsletter from "scratch" by beginning with a blank piece of paper. You will be surprised at how thick the folder can get and how your "problem" will now be choosing which pieces to write about.

3. Add personality to your newsletter. You are not just another commoditized lawyer. You have a life. You have a unique story. You might not think it is interesting, but other people will. Let them know what positions you take on matters outside of the law. Show them what's going on with your family. Do you have any other interests or hobbies? Are you a runner? Are there current events you can comment on? Let them know you are a real human being.

4. If you maintain a blog (and you should) it can become even easier to put your newsletter together at the beginning of the month. Your blog articles can become the basis for newsletter articles. Don't worry that everyone in the world is reading your blog. They aren't.

5. If you are at all uncomfortable with making a personality out of yourself (and even if you aren't) find someone else in your community to write about. Is there another small business that is doing well? Write an article about that business and then when the newsletter is published, give that business a hundred copies to place in their waiting room. Better yet, frame the copy of your newsletter with the article about them and "present" it to them and hang it up in their store/place of business.

6. Tired of writing? Have another business owner in your local community submit an article to your newsletter. I even know some attorneys who charge other businesses a fee to do this, which helps fund the cost of mailing the newsletter. Even if the other business owner doesn't have the time to write it's pretty easy to interview them (or hire someone to interview them) and write the article for them. They will love you for it.

• •

Ben's Bonus Success Tip #7

At BenGlassLaw, the entire marketing effort is centered on a unique first message:

"Before talking to the adjuster, get our free book." This message is followed by a marketing system that delivers the book and a ton of other information to them automatically and repeatedly.

You must figure out a message that stand in front of all of the other lawyers who shout *"I'm here, I'm good and I give free consultations."*

• •

7. Hire a ghostwriter. There are lots of good writers out there who would love to be on the lookout for article ideas for you and turn them into great copy.

8. Don't forget to look inside your own camera for snapshots of the kids or family. Again, in the end, people want to do business with people they like. When your raving fans understand that you are a human being they are more likely to like you. When they like you, they will hire you.

9. You can change things up every once in a while. Instead of a newsletter, send a large format postcard. You can send an "all-news" format postcard or, when you go on vacation send your fans a "wish you were here" card that looks like you bought it at the beach souvenir store.

10. Think "recycle and repurpose." Every time you write an article think of all of the other places it could be used (blog, website, letter to the editor, article for local newspaper.)

11. Submit every article you write to internet syndication sites like SubmitYourArticle.com. Not only will syndication sites blast you all over the Internet (earning valuable backlinks) but you'll also have a place to store the articles. You can then pull them out later, update them and use them again!

Exhausted by all this information? One of the benefits available to members of Great Legal Marketing is that we will do their newsletter for them, hassle free. No, it's not one of those stupid canned newsletters. It's filled with interesting articles and is 100% customizable by you. We also have access to a great printing and mailing house and we've negotiated great prices. For more information go to GLM-NewsletterForYou.com.

Keys to an Effective
LAW FIRM NEWSLETTER

- Write daily.

- Mailed monthly.

- Not devoted entirely to law.

- Personality in writing.

- Take a position—create controversy.

- "Celebretize" someone else in your community and/or staff member.

- Advertise your books/cds/dvd

- Show testimonials and show how they can give testimonials

- Refer back to your internet site and blogs.

- Also create PDF and upload to your site and "Facebook" and "Tweet" about it.

Remember, You Have a Choice.

Boring and "Lawyerlike" or Interesting and Readable

LiveLifeBigNow™ NEWSLETTER

April 2011 • Volume 15 • Number 2

a monthly publication of
Ben Glass Law

This newsletter is for informational purposes only and no legal advice is intended.

Veto Overrides Governor McDonnell's Slap in the Face to Malpractice Victims

by Ben Glass

Over the winter, patient advocates and doctors got together to craft an amendment to Virginia's horrendous medical malpractice cap. The amendment will increase the "cap" on damages from $2 million to $3 million over the next few years. Though this amendment overwhelmingly passed both sides of the General Assembly, the Governor (who is looking at a bigger national office, no doubt) vetoed it, putting personal gain over the rights of the most seriously injured in Virginia.

Fortunatey, his veto was overridden before the ink was dry. Hopefully, he and his family will never need to test the limits of one of the worst tort reform laws in the country.

(Disagree with me on this? Go ahead, you can volunteer for tort reform for your family. It's free at VolunteerForTortReform.com)

In this issue...

- Page 1 Veto Overrides Governor McDonnell's Slap in the Face to Malpractice Victims
- Page 1 Have You Downloaded Our iPhone App Yet?
- Page 2 Great Gift for Grads
- Page 2 Did You Know We Represent Kids Free?
- Page 2 A Tough Loss at Trial
- Page 2 Are You a Northern Virginia Business Owner or Entrepreneur?

We Get Questions

- **Q:** I was recently in an accident that was the other person's fault. I just received a letter from my own health insurance company asking me a bunch of questions about the accident. Do I have to respond?

- **A:** The insurance company is exploring whether they have a right of reimbursement from you out of the proceeds of your accident case. In many cases, by contract they do have that right. This is especially true if you have a group policy provided by your employer.

  There are exceptions. For example, if you have a private policy issued in Virginia, you will NOT have to pay the insurance company back. They might still send you a letter requesting information but if your policy is a private policy, you do not need to respond. (But you better be correct when judging whether you have a private policy or not.)

  Our office will be happy to review any letter you receive from your health insurance company and give you an opinion about whether money needs to be paid back. Call us.

Have You Downloaded Our iPhone App Yet?

No, we weren't the first on this one but ours is the best. (And we are getting ready to roll out an updated version.)

Right now we only have the iPhone version. We are working on the iPad version.

Go to BenGlassLawApp.com to download it if you have an iPhone.

The BenGlassLaw Newsletter

CHARLES E. BOYK LAW OFFICES NAMES
JEFF SCHLEKIE
AS GOOD NEWS, GOOD PEOPLE WINNER

Jeff Schlekie, Good News Good People Winner

Jeff Schlekie was recently chosen as the latest winner in the "Good News, Good People" Contest. Good News, Good People is a year-long program, sponsored by Charles E. Boyk Law Offices, that honors ordinary citizens who makes a positive impact in their community.

Nominated by a fellow student at the University of Toledo, Jeff was chosen because he started the organization, LitterBugz, to help clean up Toledo. Briana Edmondson states that Jeff "wanted to make a difference by starting a nonprofit organization known as the 'LitterBugz' to promote a cleaner and greener Toledo."

Jeff is a senior at the University of Toledo majoring in Marketing and Professional Sales. He wanted to start LitterBugz because he "doesn't like litter." He felt that he could clean the city with a brand, a logo, and a movement.

Jeff started off this organization by meeting with a few friends interested in the movement in his apartment. They began meeting in early March 2011 and became official on March 23, 2011. For their first event to clean up Toledo, they had 22 volunteers, and collected 28 bags of trash! The number of volunteers has grown to roughly 100 people, and Jeff hopes the number will continue to grow over the coming months.

LitterBugz meets every Saturday to pick up litter. They meet at Rocket Hall on the University of Toledo's campus and then choose a residential area to clean up for the day. They pick up litter from 2p.m-5:30p.m., with a 45 minute break where food, drinks, and entertainment is provided. "We hope to collect three to four hundred bags of trash by the end of summer," stated Jeff.

"Jeff is a smart young man who takes massive action on helping his community," said Charles E. Boyk.

We were happy to recognize Jeff for all his help and support in cleaning up Toledo! If you would like to volunteer to help clean up Toledo, please visit **www.thelitterbugz.com** for more information!

SMART PHONE SAFETY — TALK ABOUT THE E-MAIL THAT WAS SENT

It may be hard to believe, but new technology can track down you and your friends from a picture.

Pictures that you have e-mailed or uploaded from your Smartphone or Blackberry could be leaking location information and threatening your safety or that of your children. When you post pictures to your social media sites such as Facebook, Twitter, PhotoBucket, and Craigslist, it may be possible for others to discover the exact address where the photo was taken - just with a click.

How It Works

Smartphones leave a high-tech invisible trail using the same geotracking technology that enables the social website Foursquare and handheld map apps. Once you have obtained the software you can translate geotagged photos, uploaded or linked from popular websites, into maps.

How To Deactivate Your Geotagging

The site Icanstalku.com reposts pictures from unwitting Twitter users in real time, translating their photos into actual addresses and maps. The site also lists a how to deactivate geotagging on the iPhone, Blackberry with GPS, Google Android, and Palm WebOS.

The site recommends restricting which applications can access GPS marking, or turning off location services altogether in your smartphone settings.

NOMINATIONS NOW BEING ACCEPTED, VISIT goodnewsgoodpeople.com TODAY!

ABOUT "GOOD NEWS, GOOD PEOPLE"

The "Good News, Good People" contest is a year-long program sponsored by Charles E. Boyk Law Offices. Here's how it works:

- If you know someone who goes above and beyond to better their community, nominate them to win.

- Nominate anyone who has a great story to tell—the volunteer at the local food shelter who puts in more time than anyone else, the teacher who stays late to help students with homework, the child who donated his or her allowance money to charity or anyone else who makes Northwest Ohio a better place to live.

- On the first and third Monday of every month, the Charles E. Boyk Law Offices will announce one person as the newest winner and we will share their story with the community.

- Each winner will receive a prize pack valued at over $100 that is tailored to the person's story and interests. The winner will also receive a certificate commemorating their win.

- Nominators will be entered into a drawing for a "feel-good" prize of their own.

- Visit www.goodnewsgoodpeople.com to download a nomination form and to read the stories of past winners.

Mastermind Member Chuck Boyk, Toledo, OH

May 2011

BREYER LAW OFFICES

ALEXIS & MARK'S NEWS

A Little about the law–A lot about everything else!

WHAT'S INSIDE

Pg. 1 NOTE FROM ALEXIS & MARK
 • CONGRATULATIONS!
 • VICTORY OF THE MONTH

Pg. 2 EVENTS COMING UP
 • SAFETY FIRST
 • A NOTE FROM ALEXIS AND MARK

Pg. 3 A NOTE FROM ALEXIS AND MARK
 • A LITTLE ABOUT THE LAW
 • A YUMMY RECIPE

Pg. 4 RAVING FAN OF THE MONTH

A Note From Alexis & Mark

Here we are entering the summer already. It's amazing how time flies.

This past month was really busy. Mark had a trial scheduled, but it settled a couple days before the trial started. That was great news because we had gone through a mediation that was unsuccessful and then waited until trial to get a great settlement for the client. Trials always energize the office because there are so many things that need to be planned. Mark, especially, gets excited because trials are his passion. That being said, the offer was a great one so Mark lost his opportunity to try the case. We have to do what is best for the client though!

This month, the elementary school had an opportunity for parents to visit PE class (gym class) for the kids. Mark and I went to Ariella's PE class. Ariella is in 2nd grade. She was so excited to see us come into her class because we did not think we would be able to make it due to work commitments. Mark was able to move some appointments around to surprise Ariella and show up for her gym class. The PE (gym) teacher had everyone in teams and it seemed relatively non-competitive. The different groups of second graders were just having fun and doing their best. That is, it was non-competitive and simple fun until Mark got there. We got there a little late because Mark had to finish an appointment before heading to surprise Ariella at school. Well, Mark got into the relay race and immediately started telling the second graders on his team (including Ariella) how their team was going to win... meanwhile they weren't even supposed to be competing. It was just for fun and exercise for PE class. Mark had the kids in his team high fiving him and cheering each other on. Everyone knows Mark is competitive with winning cases, but even winning a second grade relay race....c'mon! *(Editor's Note from Mark: It was a close race, so I had to do some diving and sliding in my suit. Broke one button off and had to take my suit to the dry cleaners but it was worth it . . . We Won!)*

Congratulations!

Back in the beginning of the 2010-2011 school year, we were selected as the southwest regional sponsors of the Viral Video Scholarship Contest with the American Lawyer Academy. The contest was designed to spread the message of safe driving habits to teens. We received many impressive entries from Arizona, Texas, New Mexico, and Oklahoma, and after much public debate and voting, our regional winner was selected.

Congratulations to Nathan Vickery, Dual Credit Computer Graphics Teacher Christi Stuebben, and the 8th Grade Class at First Baptist Academy in Universal City, Texas! Their video, entitled, "There's a Time to Drive, and a Time to Text," was a touching story about a teen driver who makes a bad decision to text while driving, and costs the life of a child.

Now in the running for the national 1st place $10,000 scholarship or the $3,000 2nd place scholarship, the class will at least be the happy recipients of the $1,500 regional winner scholarship. National winners will be announced on June 1st. We wish our regional winner the best of luck!!

Victory Of The Month

Our client was out riding his bike in his neighborhood at night while his dog ran next to him on a leash. This was a nightly event for the dog and our client. While our client followed the leash law, his neighbor failed to do so. When the neighbor's dog saw our client coming on his bike – dog beside him – the neighbor's dog darted out in front of our client in the street.

In his attempt to avoid hitting the neighbor's dog, our client was thrown from his bike at a high speed and suffered serious injuries. The defendant's insurance company tried to deny compensation to our client but finally agreed to pay full value after we fought the case all the way to mediation – Right before trial.

Mastermind Members Mark and Alexis Breyer, Phoenix, AZ

Chapter 12

YOUR INBOUND MEDIA—CAN YOU BE FOUND WHERE THEY ARE LOOKING?

When someone decides that they need legal information they either:

1. Talk to a lawyer they already know.
2. Seek out a referral from a trusted source.
3. Go looking on the internet or yellow pages.
4. Call the last law firm they heard on the radio or saw on TV.

Your database, newsletter and persistent marketing to your "herd" locks down 1 and 2 for you. Anyone who is in your newsletter database should have you "top of mind" because you are marketing to them every month with an interesting, mailed newsletter.

If they are going to the internet or the yellow pages ("inbound media") they have choices and lots of ads "shouting" at them.

Your website or yellow page ad must:

1. Attract their attention.
2. Get them interested in what you have to say.
3. Provoke them to start the conversation with you first by raising their hand to request your free information package.
4. Get them to stop their search for another attorney until you have had the chance to let them hear your marketing message. You do this by making a "guide to hiring an attorney" a part of your information package.

(*The Truth About Lawyer Advertising* is my "guide" for consumers. TheTruthAboutLawyerAds.com

No matter whether they are using the internet or flipping phonebook pages an effective marketing system must ultimately make an offer that is so irresistible that they say to themselves "I'd be a fool to go any further in my search without raising my hand and asking for the free information this attorney is offering."

No matter which "inbound media" we are talking about the "structure" is the same.

1. **Interesting, Provocative Headline** (Get Their Attention)
2. **Copy that Enters the Conversation in Their Mind** (Speak Directly to Your Perfect Client)
3. **The Irresistible Offer** (Makes Them Identify Themselves to You)

<u>Headlines</u> (Get them to stick around and keep reading)

What do you look for when going through the newspaper? How do you decide which articles to read? The answer is that you read the headlines. The headline draws you in. The purpose of the headline is to entice you to read the first paragraph of text.

For most lawyers, the headline of the ad is something like

"Personal Injury"

or

"Hurt? We Can Help"

or

"We Care For You"

or (worse)

"Your Name"

or (even worse)

"Your Firm Name"

Not only are these headlines not interesting but they are exactly the same headlines that all of the other attorneys are using. Why would they even start reading your ad? (Remember, successful entrepreneurs look around, see what everyone else is doing, and do something different!)

Do you think your ad just might have a better chance of being read if the headline, instead of saying something like "personal injury" said:

"Five Deadly Sins that Can Wreck Your Accident Case"

"What's So Special About a Free Consultation in a Personal Injury Case?"

"Is You Doctor Making These Mistakes With Your Disability Case?"

"DWI-what Your Lawyer Doesn't Know Can Hurt You"

"Why Most Medical Malpractice Victims Never Recover a Dime"

How to Guarantee that Your Disability Claim Will Be Denied

<u>Copy</u> (Keep them interested)

Most lawyers make the mistake of beginning their ad copy by talking about themselves. Go ahead, check out the ads and websites yourself. Most lawyer ads are some version of:

> **"We have been practicing law for a combined total of 20 years. We went to_____ Law School. We are members of XYZ Associations and are honored to be included in "America's Most Stupendous Lawyers." We have achieved great success for our clients."**

To the extent the ad has any graphics they usually include:

1. A logo they love.
2. A picture of a gavel or courthouse
3. A picture of themselves
4. A picture of the skyline of their city or
5. (gasp) A picture of the inside of their conference room.

I created this "badge."
Email me and you too
can be a Super Duper
Lawyer of the Galaxy.

I guarantee you that someone who woke up this morning to begin the process of (1) finding out more about their problem or (2) finding the right lawyer for their case didn't say to themselves **"I wonder what law school Ben Glass went to and what associations he belongs to?"**

Nope.

They had a problem they needed solving. They have concerns that they believe may result in a need to hire an attorney. Imagine how powerful your ad world be if the reader — *your perfect client* — felt that the ad was written just for them — You know how to do this because you solve these problems all day long.

Here are some examples of copy that "Enters the conversation going on in the prospect's mind."

If you've been in an accident you probably have questions:

1. **Who will pay my bills?**
2. **Which doctor should I see?**
3. **Should I send my doctor bills to my health insurance company?**
4. **Who will repair my car?**

You may not need an attorney but I've answered these questions and more in my new book [insert your book title.]

Or

Did you know that a respected Federal Judge once said that a claimant who does not have an attorney when filing a disability claim may be at a significant disadvantage later? That another said that ERISA-the law that controls employee disability claims-Really stands for "Everything Ridiculous Invented Since Adam?" Insurance companies know that most claimants will not be able to find an experienced ERISA disability attorney...

• •

Ben's Bonus Success Tip #8

When you see people who are successful, ask them these three questions:

1. What do you think made you successful?
2. How did you know how to do that?
3. How can I use that in my practice?

• •

Provoking Them To Start a Conversation With Us (Making the Irresistible Offer)

Most lawyer ads have no call to action other than a "call us now for a free consultation." Nothing very special (or compelling) about that, is there? You need to be different.

You need to have a way to get "in front of" all of those ads whose only call to action is the phone call.

The single best way to do this is to provide some sort of information resource such as a book or free report that provides the answers to the questions that you know are going through their mind. You want to create an "information premium" that the prospective client will literally be *compelled* to request before proceeding further.

In fact, becoming the "one who wrote the book on [your practice area] solves two obvious problems for you:

1. It gives prospects a really good reason to identify themselves to you and "start a conversation" and
2. It starts to establish you as the expert in your field, far better than a laundry list of years in practice, societies invited into and schools attended.

Here's the goal with your offer: Have the prospect conclude that "I'd be a fool to talk to the adjuster/hire an attorney/handle this case on my own without at least requesting the information the attorney is offering."

The Non-Obvious Problem—Solved

Designing print ads and websites that have as their purpose the goal of making the irresistible offer also have the additional benefit of not making your ad "try to do too much"

Most lawyer ads try to make the "complete sale." They bend over backwards trying to convince the reader that the lawyer/firm is to be hired right now on the basis of this one marketing piece! It's like making a marriage proposal on the first date! That's a lot to ask!

Designing a focused ad whose only purpose is to provoke the request for the book is a far simpler task. To make matters even better, when you design ads that are about "the book" (instead of "we care for you") you operate in a virtual "competition free zone." Think about the possibilities when the ad is for your book and not for legal services: the headlines, offers, guarantees and testimonials are almost endless when we first market a (free) consumer book and not our legal services. As you design you next ad (after you write your book) ask yourself this question: "What does the ad need to say to make people request the book?" For more information about what it means to market in a "competition free zone" visit www.CompetitionFreeZone.com.

So, Ben, when does the "sale" occur?

The sale to your best clients will occur after the prospective client arrives at the conclusion in their own mind, <u>after your follow up marketing</u>, that you are the wise man/woman at the top of the mountain.

Five Deadly Sins That Can Wreck Your Virginia Accident Case
(Avoid Them and You Just May Have A Chance)

This new free book, written by an attorney with 22 years' experience battling the insurance companies, will arm you with the inside secrets you need before hiring a lawyer or dealing with the insurance company on your own. If you have been injured in an accident, you should read this valuable information before calling for the first "free consultation." (You know, the one that everyone offers "free," like it's some big deal.)

Ben Glass says he wrote this book because he is *"sick and tired of insurance companies taking advantage of people before they have access to this information."*

After sitting down in your own home and reading this book, you'll know: Why a quick settlement can be a GIANT mistake. What "service" provided by some lawyers can be the kiss of death to your case. Why some lawyers insist that a one-third fee (or "gulp" 40%) is "standard" while others charge as little as 15% of the recovery. What it means when lawyers advertise that they are Board Certified or listed in Best Lawyers in America.

This Free Book Reveals:

• What document you should never sign for an insurance company
• Why a local judge called a chiropractor a "hired gun" after the claimant's lawyer committed one of the "Five Deadly Sins" of a personal injury case
• How to prevent your past from coming back to destroy your personal injury case
• Why your health insurance company may claim your **ENTIRE RECOVERY** for itself
• What terms like "no fee if no recovery" really mean
• How to really *read* lawyer advertising
• 10 specific steps you can take to find the best lawyer for your case

You can get a free copy of *Five Deadly Sins That Can Wreck Your Virginia Accident Case* by calling 800-561-1670 ext. 253 anytime, 24 hours a day, and simply following the prompts, by calling our office at 703-591-9829, or by visiting the website below.

www.5DeadlySins.com

Notice—Dense copy and no graphics. "But Ben, they won't read it all!"

Sure they will, if it is interesting and they think you are talking about them.

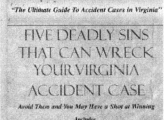
Notice that the ad is all about the book, not the lawyer!

Chapter 13

YELLOW PAGE MARKETING—
STILL KICKING (IN SOME PLACES)

Let me first be clear that I think in most places the Yellow Pages is a dying media. I've noticed that hotels don't even stock them anymore. I don't know that I have personally used the Yellow Pages in years and my children certainly don't. That being said, there *are* still some areas of the country where Great Legal Marketing members are still getting a decent return on investment with their yellow page advertising. I understand that there are still some places in the country where the only way to access the Internet is through a dial-up modem. Interestingly, we now have anecdotal evidence of salespeople making deals for yellow page space so good the ads are tempting. With lawyers bailing on the Yellow Pages at an ever-increasing rate your ad now has a better opportunity to stand out.

In the end the only way to know for sure if the Yellow Pages ads are working is to run a creative direct response driven ad and track it intimately. As long as it pays for itself and adds names to your raving fan base and you don't have a better use of your dollar, then go for it.

If you are going to advertise in the Yellow Pages, please don't let the ad rep design your ad. He will want to make it look just like all of the other ads. Forget the gavels, eagles, flags and courthouse scenes. None of that will make your ad stand out and compel a prospect to contact you first.

Remember the keys (and the reps will fight you all of the way on this.)

1. Compelling headline. This is not your firm name or something meaningless like "Divorce Attorney."
2. Plenty of interesting copy that "enters the conversation in the prospect's mind." (The reps will tell you that white space sells. Just think about that statement for a minute!)
3. An irresistible offer. The reader of your ad should come to the conclusion that they would be silly to take another step with their legal problem before at least looking at what you are offering (book, CD, free report, DVD) for free.

When you register this book at **RegisterTheBook.com** I'll send you a ton of yellow page ad samples created by Great Legal Marketing Members.

Chapter 14

EFFECTIVE FOLLOW UP — THE HIDDEN SECRET

Note from Ben: At BenGlassLaw, we monitor all of our leads and, in particular, the length of time between incident date and first contact with our office, and then the time from initial contact date with our office to signed fee agreement. We then correlated this information with severity of injury/size of case. Know what we found? For our largest cases it is typically several months between incident and inquiry and four months to a year between initial inquiry with our office (usually via a request for one of our books at the website) and signed fee agreement.

Do you know how many times we initiated contact with that prospect in just the first six months that they were in our system? 14!! Even more if we found out their birth date or anniversary.

Now, consider this thought-If the prospective client has contacted several firms at the same time as they initially contacted us, how many of those firms were still marketing to them at all after the first contact? How many times would you have marketed to them in that time period? How many cases are you missing because you give up too easily?

As you might imagine, this type of follow up marketing is almost impossible without a system that does it for you automatically.

My friends Clate Mask and Scott Martineau have created software that is <u>the system</u> for automating your follow up marketing. You can see a video of how BenGlassLaw uses Infusionsoft to automate not only the marketing but the case management at our firm at **www.GLM-Software.com.**

I've asked Clate and Scott, who have helped thousands of small businesses around the world automate their follow up marketing, to contribute a chapter about this vital, most almost always overlooked, marketing strategy.

The Hidden Secret of Really Great Legal Marketing

By Clate Mask & Scott Martineau, Founders of Infusionsoft

Rather than beat around the bush, I want to get straight to the point and reveal **one of the most powerful secrets for growing your practice**.

In fact, of all the marketing and sales techniques you've heard, one will have a bigger impact on your business than any other strategy you might use. So what is the secret?

*If you want to experience rapid, profitable growth, you must **follow up consistently and effectively with ALL of your prospects and clients**.*

You must be standing there the moment someone needs your services. You need to respond quickly when a past client makes a referral. And you better be on you're A-game the moment a prospect finally turns to you for help. But why is follow-up so important? Why is it the one thing that causes you to stand out from your competitors and drives more revenue to your bank account?

It all goes back to one basic marketing principle:

People Buy When They Are Ready to Buy

Unlike many consumer goods and services, no one hires an attorney "just because." Hiring legal counsel is not an impulse decision. No one is going to seek your services…unless they need you. But just because a prospect doesn't need legal services at this precise moment, doesn't mean they won't need them in the future.

If you've been following up with ALL your prospects and clients, guess who's getting a phone call when that need arises. You! And here's why:

1. <u>You're Building Relationships of Trust</u>

Let's face it- attorneys don't have the best reputation. The first time you speak with a prospective client, they're assessing your personality. They are sizing you up; waiting for you to reveal your shark teeth.

However, if you've kept in constant communication with your prospects, you've done what your competition only wishes they could do. You've already built a relationship of trust with your contacts. In place of distrust and skepticism, you've built loyalty and security. And guess what? When your prospects need legal counsel (and they will) they'll immediately track you down. (No matter what your competitors might be offering.)

2. You're Keeping Your Name Fresh in Your Contacts' Mind

As great as your services might be, your prospects and past clients are not sitting around thinking about you. They're busy, and they've got other things on their minds. They're thinking about work, grocery shopping, where the kids are, etc. In fact, your past clients may have even forgotten your name!

So when the need for law services arises, chances are, your prospects aren't thinking about you at all. At the family reunion, when someone mentions lawyers, your past clients don't immediately think of mentioning your name. Unless…you successfully remind your contacts of who you are, what you do, and how your services are better than your competitors.

With consistent, effective follow-up, you never give your contacts a chance to forget about you. If **anything**, law related comes up, you're the first person your contacts think about.

3. You're Building the Loyalty of Your Clients and Prospects

The last benefit of keeping in touch with your contacts is: no one else is doing it. It's too hard. For the rookie attorney with only a handful of contacts, following up with people is easy. But the longer you're in business, the more difficult it becomes.

However, if you're taking the time to reach out to your contacts, they're going to feel it. And they'll appreciate it. You see, the primary reason clients don't refer friends, or give you repeat business, is because they don't feel appreciated. They feel as though they are one-of-many. Why should they think of you when, often the case is over, you act like you never think about them?

But you have the power to change all that. With simple follow-up, you can make your clients feel as though **they are your only priority**. And who wouldn't recommend service like that?

So What Happens When There's Not Enough of YOU to Go Around?

If you've been in business very long, you've come to many of these conclusions yourself. You undoubtedly understand the value of consistent follow-up. But like most small business owners, you've stretched yourself too far as it is. How are you supposed to constantly follow up with all of your prospects and customers on top of everything else you've got to do?

It's not tough to figure out that the number one reason small business owners fail to follow up with clients and prospects is the lack of time. It's not an easy thing to run your business AND keep in touch with all your contacts.

Unless… you automate your business.

With automated technology, it's easy to instantly send multi-step, multi-media, follow-up sequences to exactly the right person at exactly the right time; and to create powerful, effective messages by personalizing those campaigns.

Let me give you an example of how this would work. Imagine you're an estate planning attorney and a potential client winds up on your website. They want to create a will and need an attorney. Right now, they're in the process of "researching" their options. In an attempt to capture online leads, you've included a free report on your website entitled, "How to Draft Your Own Will (and Cut Down on Your Attorney Fees)." In exchange for someone's name, phone number, and email address, you're willing to part with an exclusive, valuable report.

The visitor is interested, so they sign up for the report. And since you understand the benefits of automation, rather than tracking their request, finding and sending the report, and following up with a phone call in a few days, you decide to let your automated follow-up marketing system take over. After all, you don't have the time to be constantly sending off free reports anyway.

Once this visitor fills out the web form with their personal information, your automated system kicks in. Instantly the new prospect is directed to a webpage that says, "Congratulations, your free report is being sent to the email address you gave us." (So far you don't have to do anything.)

The prospect goes to their email and finds the report. They like it. They appreciate the information you freely shared, and they are a little bit more interested in your firm. But not interested enough to take action yet. They're still looking at other options.

That's okay. You've got a plan. With an automated system at your disposal, the new prospect gets a "personal" email from you the next day. It says: *Hey, I hope you enjoyed the free report. Did you know a will is invalid if it's not properly created and witnessed?* And you send them more educational materials to go along with it. (As well as your contact information.)

Okay, you just moved this prospect to SERIOUS interest stage. Now whether the person requests your services at this moment or not is immaterial. With an automated process you can continue to send **predetermined, prewritten, personalized** letters, emails, faxes, postcards, and, when appropriate, voice broadcasts to this prospect for years to come and, following a well-known marketing "truth," this person will call you when they're ready.

The more you can keep the communication flowing, the better off you're going to be. With the power of automation you can keep in touch with every single contact on your list...without adding more work to your busy schedule!

Please visit www.GLM-Software.com to learn more about how Ben Glass uses Infusionsoft to run a very complex and effective follow-up marketing campaign.

Infusionsoft, the leader in marketing automation software for entrepreneurs and small businesses is revolutionizing the way small businesses grow. The company's integrated marketing automation software helps business owners convert prospects to customers, get repeat sales, and grow their business without growing staff.

(Clate and Scott are also the authors of *Conquer the Chaos: How to Grow a Successful Small Business Without Going Crazy*. It is available at Amazon and should be on your "must read" list.)

Great LEGAL MARKETING

The BIGGEST MISTAKES
You Are Making With
Your Marketing Part 2

- Letting the *marketing vulture* (who has no incentive to make you stand out amongst all the other lawyers they are selling space to) design your ad.

- Failure to accept that , yes, indeed, it is OK to run a law firm as a *profitable business* and, in fact, that should be your highest goal.

- Failure to develop *marketing pieces* that are designed to attract that PERFECT client to YOUR PERFECT practice.

- Failing to really *cultivate your raving fans* so that they do more of your marketing for you.

- Failure to develop and manage an effective *database of raving fans.*

- Failing to invest time and money in *learning about marketing.*

- Failure to define what makes up the *perfect practice* for YOU.

- Failure to identify and define the *perfect client* for YOU.

Chapter 15

THE INTERNET—AN INTRODUCTION
Today's Primary Inbound Marketing Media

Note from Ben: This chapter is for those who outsource all of their Internet marketing. Even if you are paying someone else to run your entire Internet marketing operation you need to understand the best strategy and technology to use in order to communicate effectively with your webmaster. You can end up spending a ton of money on someone who makes a very pretty website but delivers no cases. Frankly, most webmasters are not marketing experts at all. They are good at designing websites, but have no clue what is really involved in generating attorney marketing that is effective. That's like buying an expensive car and leaving it in the driveway.

Since 1995, my webmaster has been Tom Foster of Foster Web Marketing. You can find him and review his portfolio of clients at FosterWebMarketing.com.

For many members of Great Legal Marketing, the Internet has become a marketing engine. Others struggle because they lack a comprehensive plan and they have not teamed with a technology partner to maximize the Internet as a marketing tool. Internet marketing is much more than a mere ego driven website. While page one positioning on Google is vital—it's still not enough.

Numerous legal marketing commentators suggest that websites and blogs are used to establish yourself as a "thought leader" in the <u>hope</u> that a consumer will figure this fact out, search you out and initiate contact. Hope is not a good strategy. This belief is yet another example of the "work your way up the ladder of success" and "do good work and they will come" mentality that has pervaded lawyer marketing since advertising was first allowed.

• •

Ben's Bonus Success Tip #9

Forget the "ladder of success." No "rules" mandate that you climb the same ladder that everyone else wants to climb.

• •

Let me be clear. The Internet has one purpose. Your websites, blogs and any other impression that you have on the cyberspace world should provoke the visitor to initiate contact with you. In fact, let me make it even easier than that. Anything you do on the Internet should be designed to have the client say "I'd be a fool to talk to [the adjuster/hire an attorney/sign any forms] before I request the free information that [you, the lawyer] are offering." (Do you see a principle emerging here?)

The Internet is just another form of media. Your message doesn't change much just because the Internet is the media. While promoting yourself on your website as an authority is laudable and certainly should not be ignored, you will get beat every time by someone who is using the Internet as the front edge of a comprehensive marketing program. This is why the "be a thought leader and they will come" gurus are wrong. You need to get the consumer to raise their hand and to say to you "I'm interested in hearing more of what you have to say."

In order to have an effective Internet presence that encourages the consumer to initiate contact with you, your Internet site must do the following:

1. Dominate the search engine return page (SERP) so that you are "everywhere."
2. Create interest with a compelling headline. This can be delivered by video. This is <u>not</u> your name, your logo or a picture of your city.
3. Maintain interest long enough for the consumer to see your "irresistible offer" and get them to click on it or get the consumer to submit a question together with contact information to you.
4. Automatically take the new contact information and put it into your database and kick off a multistep multimedia sequence of marketing events.

How Any Lawyer Can Dominate Google

Obtaining and maintaining a commanding presence on Google requires both technology and a willingness to work. Make no mistake about how competitive and difficult it is to achieve a prominent position on the first page of Google. However, once you do it can be very difficult to knock you off and it is disheartening for your competitors. The best attorney internet marketers can usually achieve more than one position on the first page of Google (without buying expensive Adwords).

Here are the technology essentials:

1. <u>A website content management tool.</u> Gone are the days when you hire a webmaster and every time you want to change or add content to your website you call the webmaster, wait for weeks, and finally see the change. Whoever is designing and maintaining your website should have a "backdoor," or content management system that you can access on the fly to create and upload:
    a. New pages
    b. New content on existing pages
    c. New frequently asked questions
    d. New practice areas
    e. New images and photographs
    f. Blog entries
    g. News that is appropriate to your practice area
    h. PDF documents including court opinions, briefs and your mailed, monthly law firm newsletter
    i. Video (That is then itself automatically pushed to the various video distribution sites on the internet.)
    j. Contact forms and information request forms that automatically add contacts to your contact database.

If you do not have a content management system that allows you to do these activities then your website will never keep up. While Google consistently changes the way it perceives and then ranks the utility of websites one thing remains clear-fresh new content remains king. Many lawyers are now employing writers and bloggers to constantly and consistently push good relevant content to the Internet. The top performing websites are "media machines" and the attorneys behind them consider themselves "publishers."

Too much work? Life is a choice. You can keep buying those static template websites from the mega website designers, but you cannot continue to complain when the sites fail to produce cases for you.

2. <u>You need software that tracks the actual search terms that people are using to come to your site</u>. Google Analytics is a free tool that every website should have and if your web designer has not included this tool in your package and shows you how to use it you should pick up the phone and fire them. This is important because while lawyers are willing to spend a ton of money bidding for "vanity" keywords like "Virginia personal injury attorney" yet over 70% of all searches do not use the vanity keywords. Most searches are in the form of a question or some sort of an extended statement. It is absolutely vital that you know what the 70% of non-vanity keywords are that are being used to find you in order that you can create more content optimized for those "long-tail keywords" to "feed" Google.

Your Website Should Be Driving Clients to You While You Play

Special Bonus: want to see a 'tour' of some really crappy attorney websites and wasted money on Google AdWords? I've got a cool video that will upset web development companies and lawyers alike

at **MyAttorneyWebsiteSucks.com.**

Chapter 16

OVERALL INTERNET STRATEGY
(What *NOT* to Do)

Once you have the technology in place, you can implement your strategy. Remember, the purpose of the website is simply to get consumers to "raise their hand" by clicking on one of the buttons that has them either requesting information from you or telling you about their case. With that in mind, let's start first with some of the mistakes that lawyers make and you may be making right now with your website.

1. Devoting the top third of your main page to useless things like your firm logo, a picture of you, the firm name or a picture of the city you're in. Here's the problem. This looks just like every other lawyer marketing website out there. Remember what we said: be different. Shout a different message. When a consumer lands on your website you literally have seconds to grab their attention to keep them reading. You need a compelling headline with copy that keeps their interest. Some of the top performing sites include video as part of that "headline."

2. Writing about you. I guarantee you that a consumer looking for a lawyer did not wake up this morning wondering where you went to law school or how many years you have been practicing. Instead, they wonder about the problems they are having. Your headline and copy must enter the conversation going on in their mind. No matter what your niche practice area, you know what your clients tell you when they come in to hire you. You know the fears, questions and concerns they have. Your copy (and your video) must answer these concerns. It is a huge waste of time to

be telling them on the first page about how many jury trials you've had. They don't care.

3. Forgetting about the headlines and copy on all of the internal pages of your website. Remember, when your web presence is done effectively, consumers may be "entering" your website at any of thousands of your pages. Each page that you create must be crafted with the principles set forth above in mind. You must always be thinking "if they landed on this page would I be able to attract their attention, keep their interest and convince them to click on a request for information?"

4. Having "contact us now" as the only way for someone to initiate contact. You must have a "widget" in the form of a book or free report at your site. Those lawyers who have been implementing the strategy for years and who back that strategy up with a multistep multimedia marketing campaign have an endless flow of new cases to choose from.

5. Failing to have a "Live Chat" box on your site. Look around. Many commercial sites have now added an additional way for consumers to "start the conversation." Of course, if you are going to implement Live Chat you must devote time and other resources to training someone to be the Live Chat operator, Remember that the purpose of the Live Chat box is simply to move the prospect further along the path of "starting the conversation with you- either by requesting your book, moving to a live phone conversation or emailing you a message about their case.

6. Not optimizing the site for the search engines. Tom Foster talks in more detail about this in the next chapter but while most lawyers know what a key word is, you should also be familiar with and understand the words "title tag" and "meta description." Each page of your site must have a unique "title tag" and "meta description" which is focused on the key words that you are optimizing that page for.

Fairfax, Virginia - **Best** Personal Injury **Car** Accident Attorney ...
Free Consumer Books on **Virginia** Personal Injury and **car accident** claims are available to **Virginia** residents before you talk to the insurance adjuster.
www.vamedmal.com/ - Cached - Similar   **Meta Description**

Fairfax, Virginia - **Best** Personal Injury **Car** Accident Attorney ...   **Title Tag**
Free Consumer Books on **Virginia** Personal Injury and **car accident** claims are available to **Virginia** residents before you talk to the insurance adjuster.
www.vamedmal.com/ - Cached - Similar

Chapter 17
STOP WHINING: MAKING YOUR WEBSITE REALLY WORK FOR YOU
By: Tom Foster, Foster Web Marketing

Note from Ben: Internet technology and opportunities seems to change almost on the fly. Remember MySpace? It was all the rage for awhile. This is why we spend considerable time at our conferences, on coaching calls and the newsletter discussing and dissecting the 'latest and greatest' Internet tool. It's funny, though, to see some state bar group do a "How can Lawyers Benefit from Facebook" seminar about a year and a half after we first spent a considerable amount of time on it at one of our conferences. Of course, the state bar event was really all about how to NOT use Facebook.

As more and more people rely on the Web to find quality legal representation, law firms and solo attorneys must look for ways to optimize their websites for high rankings on search engines—the first step in attracting more visitors and prospects. But you are a fool to rely on this alone in getting the cases you want.

While making your site easy for search engines to find and index can help drive a successful Web marketing strategy, appealing to both search engines and human readers at the same time can be challenging. The fact is that it takes more than increased website traffic to drive your firm's marketing goals.

Relevant content on your website delivers pertinent, local, timely information and emotionally connects visitors to your firm. Developing content that evokes a positive response from site visitors is the first goal. Translating that positive association into action (completing a web form, ordering a book or calling the firm)— and signing the prospects as a client—is the next. Also consider that you want the prospective client to STOP LOOKING for other lawyers. You should provide content and have all the frequently asked questions on your website for the kind of cases you want. Even if it is not exactly the case you want—you still have the lead and perhaps a referral. Nothing is wasted.

To achieve these goals, your site must feature content that not only attracts and engages humans, but also registers optimally with search engines and the "spiders or robots" they use to crawl and index your website. Appealing to both spiders and humans is not easy. The spiders are driven by logic and algorithms, and humans by emotion and personal preferences and needs. I am going to give you an easy-to-follow, three-step process for creating meaningful content that can deliver higher search engine rankings while at the same time engaging human beings and ultimately influencing a CALL TO ACTION.

● ●

Ben's Bonus Success Tip #10

Live Life Big: Your playing small does not serve the world.

Whenever you are in your philosophical or religious beliefs, I want to truly tell you this truth. You were born with a unique set of gifts and talents, and it is my personal view, as a Christian, that I have gifts and talents. I believe that what I am asked to do in my time in the world, is to maximize the use of my gifts and talents and to do what I can to make them better, to make them stronger and then to bring them to the world.

● ●

Search Engine Optimization: Voodoo Science and Creativity

It is important to first understand that Search Engine Optimization (SEO) is a complex mix of voodoo and creativity. Top search engine providers like Google, Yahoo and MSN closely guard their indexing algorithms and change them frequently. They do not share this information with the public or invite anyone into their laboratory to show them exactly how to do it either. Search engine "spiders and robots" are choosy about what they read, how they crawl through a site, how often they do it, how fast they go through the site, and finally what they choose to index.

No wonder so many attorneys and law firms turn to professional SEO consultants for help.

Yet, all of the strategizing in the world over meta keywords and domain names won't provide a foundation for effective search engine optimization alone. The mix of voodoo and creativity requires the incorporation of relevant key search phrases that tell search engines what your site is about. Whatever you are listing in your meta keyword list should also be found in meaningful content that educates, inspires, and elicits responses from site visitors.

Step One: Determining the Best Key Phrases to Draw the Visitors You Want

When it comes to web content, **search engine spiders and robots** (being extremely logical and impatient) want to crunch all of your content down into short form keywords and keyword phrases. From these minimal terms, they make determinations and inferences about the information contained on your website-and its appropriateness for different searchers.

The world of keywords is constantly changing and search engines are frequently changing their algorithms. Nonetheless, any discussion of creating content for a website that you want to rank high on the search engine indexes must start with keywords. You should consider keywords as a guide or an index of what you want searchers to find you for. You should have a unique set of keywords for each page of your website and that set of keywords should be reflective of the content that is on that specific page.

As a General Rule for Small Law Firms Use "Key Phrases", Not "Key Words"

For the most part, popular keywords identify who you are and what you do, but most stand-alone words are too broad and vague to produce good results for a small business owner or law firm. Therefore, it's best to look for specific key phrases, rather than keywords. Let's say you want to get medical malpractice cases. "Malpractice," "medical malpractice," and "surgical errors" will all produce huge numbers of listings, but still won't attract highly targeted prospect clients if used alone. The phrases "Texas medical malpractice attorney" or "Dallas surgical error attorney," however, will produce a more targeted group of listings and therefore higher-quality prospects.

Selecting Key Phrases Specific About What You Want to Do

You are in control of your own destiny and the kind of cases you get from the Web. But you must choose your path and your target wisely and stick to it. For search engines to see a site as relevant, you must use phrases that closely identify with the unique attributes of what your firm can offer. At the same time, you also must use the most popular phrases that searchers use. Lay people don't search for legal terms—other lawyers do. That's why no one gets a bunch of prospects when optimizing for "product liability attorney" or "premises liability attorney." Sure, you may get listed, but how many lay people know what this even means? More specific keyword phrases to try and optimize for would be "ACME baby crib attorney" or "slipped in Wal-mart attorney." These phrases may sound silly, but normal people searching for help are not always logical and don't use the same legal vernacular attorneys do to find information. A balance between popularity and specificity works best here.

There are two easy ways to know exactly what search terms people are using: Google Analytics and software programming which tells you what search terms someone used to fill out a form at your site. Your webmaster should already have implemented these tools for your site but if he or she has not, just show them this page!

Play reporter. Most successful search engine marketing experts that rely on organic placement agree and advise their clients to think like a reporter and employ the three w's: who, what and where. We would add to this journalistic technique a why, when and how. If your keywords can answer these questions, you've taken a big step toward success. Remember, people search *where* they are, *what* they want, and *who* they want it from. When is always NOW.

Consider motivation. In addition to popularity and specificity, motivation should be a consideration in key phrase selection as well. Someone searching for "Atlanta 85 car wreck attorney" has a different motivation from someone searching for "Atlanta birth defect attorney." Your supporting content for these terms must be clear AND engaging in order to be effective and ultimately produce a CALL TO ACTION.

Another important aspect of SEO for attorney websites is that you have to understand that no one cares about you or your accomplishments (except your case results)! Your bio is meaningless to everyone else but you, your lawyer peers, your family, and your competition. Who cares what school you went to? Because you went to Yale, does this mean you can try a car accident case better than someone else? Do you care if the CEO of the software you use dropped out of Harvard? The truth is that you need to identify with the person searching for your help. They will see all your diplomas and certificates in your office when they sign your fee agreement.

Evaluate popularity and competitiveness. The next step of key phrase selection is researching their popularity and competitiveness. If you're working with a search engine optimization firm, they can guide you through this process. If you are new to search this step can be daunting. In fact, helping you research and choose effective key phrases is one of the areas where search engine optimization firms can be of most value.

Whether you choose to use a SEO firm or not, it is important to understand what 'popularity' and 'competitiveness' mean with regard to key phrase selection. 'Popularity' refers to the number of searches done by search engine users (your potential clients) of a key phrase during a particular period of time. 'Competitiveness' refers to the number of pages that are optimized for that particular key phrase.

If you just started your website or if you're trying to improve your firm's current website, you will want to look for key phrases that have the right balance between 'popularity' and 'competitiveness.' You are looking for the 'sweet spot.' You *don't* want to try to optimize your site for the most competitive keyword phrase regardless of how popular it is. You will have your most success finding a popular keyword phrase that has the least amount of competition.

So how do you find out how competitive a keyword phrase is? There are lots of tools available for you online but there is a simple easy way to do this. Go to Google and type:

intitle: keyword phrase

or

inanchor: keyword phrase

Here are some examples.

The number you see there is the number of pages Google has indexed that have optimized for that keyword.

Study your competitors. Visit sites with similar services to see what key phrases they use. Ask people-including your clients-what terms they might use if they were looking for your services. The phrases your clients use to seek legal services (and the phrases they used to find you) can be the most effective key phrases for your website.

Match your clients' language. Leave the legal jargon in the courtroom and use the language your clients use to define your service. If you're choosing key phrases like "premises liability attorney," while potential clients are searching for "slipped and broke a hip at Houston Starbucks," you may have a problem, Houston…(note to all of you "truck accident litigation" attorneys: your potential client was in a <u>car</u>. Think about that for a moment. Thinking like a lawyer is probably the last thing you want to do here!)

View Your Website Reports for Trends. A common oversight is to not utilize the resources that you have. Your website reports, which show among other things, visitor count hits and "most frequently visited 'pages.'– also provide vital keyword and phrases information to you. If there are some pages that attract a lot of visitors you should be creating more pages/videos/ free reports that are like those pages.

"Test drive" your list. Once you have a list of possibilities, search the key phrases to see what results they produce, and research those listings as well. By now, you should have a solid list of key phrases that can be tested for viability. Both Google's AdWords and Yahoo! Search Marketing have tools to help you evaluate potential keyword traffic. In addition, research tools, such as Web Position (WebPosition.com), can be helpful here as well.

Consider a small pay-per-click campaign as a test: Pay-per-click programs, such as those offered by Google or Yahoo, are often an effective, yet expensive way to test keywords. For example, you can easily buy the keywords "Orlando slip and fall attorney" "Orlando premises liability attorney" and "fell in Orlando Starbucks" to see if there are differences in quantity and quality of response. The first 2 are shotgun approaches and will likely cost the most, as more searches will be done on those terms. (Interestingly, these searches are probably mostly being done by attorneys or SEO consultants working for attorneys!) The later key phrase is a sniper approach that may not yield quantity, but could land you that big case.

In less than a month, you can have results that feed back into your site's new content plan. The same information might take three to six months to gather if you had to wait for a natural search optimization campaign alone to show results. Since it is difficult to optimize any one page for too many variations of the same word, many firms combine paid placement (Google Adwords) and organic placement—just as they might combine paid advertising with "free" editorial coverage.

Step Two: Integrate Your Key Phrases into the Site

Now that you have selected your key phrases, it's time to begin optimizing. First, ask yourself what key message and information you want to deliver with every page-and what action you want readers to take. For an existing site, determine which pages can be completed with the addition of key phrases, and which ones must be rewritten. Determine where you can add pages with relevant content for the insertion of very popular search terms, delivering more information to prospective buyers and increasing your optimization

Get specific. Many times, adding key phrases, can be as simple as substituting the key phrase for copy that is more general. For example, instead of saying: "Smith Law Firm can handle all medical malpractice cases", use "Michigan Attorneys from the Smith Law Firm take on malpractice cases such as birth defects, surgical errors, and brain injury." This approach enables you to use your key phrases more often without seeming to be repetitive.

Be a "generous cook"— sprinkle your key phrases liberally. Be creative and look for a variety of ways to use key phrases throughout your site, not only in body copy, but also in headlines, subheads, tags, and descriptions. If you're not familiar with developing tags and descriptions for your site, hire a professional or spend some time with your webmaster explaining your objectives and what the project entails. Make sure they give you what you need and that you understand.

Hit every page. You're going to need one or two key phrases for most of the pages on your website. You may not be able to uniquely optimize every page, but you should strive to. The home page and practice areas are critical, "library" articles (that include supportive content to the practice areas you are advertising for) are musts; resources or links, press releases, frequently asked questions, and other content-rich pages are usually fairly simple to optimize, so include them as well. Even the pages that are video tutorials about a consumer legal topic should have the transcripts of your words appearing on the same page as the video.

Average 2-3 key phrases per 250 words. Experts disagree on the right ratio of keywords to total words, but the consensus seems to be that you should use each key phrase two or three times per 250 words of copy. You don't want to stuff as many keywords as you can onto one page. Google does not like this. Repetition has no purpose and gives a bad impression of your company and can get you banned from search engines—two outcomes you certainly don't want.

Use headlines and subheads. Most pages have two headlines, a primary headline at the top of the page that is usually in a font size that is the biggest on the page, and a secondary header in the middle of the page that serves to break up copy and make it attractive to read. Each header should contain one of the key phrases for the page. As a general rule, keep the primary headline to six words or less, and the secondary headline to eight words or less. Make sure both headlines are written to interest both humans and spiders.

Avoid flash and graphics in headlines you want searched. Traditional search engines don't read animations or graphics. Any text embedded in an animation or a graphic on your site will be ignored by the spiders unless you provide alt text tags for the graphics. Of course, every site needs to look attractive for its human readers. You need to understand that graphics, animations, and video are not put on a site for SEO purposes, but to make your site stand-out once a visitor comes there. All content and text is good for spiders, but bad for humans. Just make sure you also include plenty of content rich in key phrases for the spiders' reading enjoyment.

It is important to note here that we are speaking in terms of traditional searches and not new emerging opportunities with technologies brought to us by Google Image Search and Google Video Search. This is an entirely new way of looking at SEO (as are the new engines themselves.)

• •

Ben's Bonus Success Tip #11

Most people are not working hard. They might do a lot of "stuff," but they are not engaged in productive work. They're spending their time on Twitter and Facebook, and watching reruns of American Idol. If someone followed you around for a week, would they say at the end of that time period, "it's no wonder how successful he is, look at all he gets done?"

• •

Think "Above the Fold." In newspapers, the stories that are most important are always at the top of the page—above the fold—on the front page or if they can't be on the front page—their title is listed on the front page. Search engines also assume the most important information about your firm is at the top, just like human readers do. Whenever possible, make sure your key phrases are used in the first few sentences of body copy. Use news stories as a guideline. Reporters start with the most critical information first and work their way down through the details. Try to use one key phrase in sentence one and the other in sentence two if possible. Remember that with headlines you are "optimizing" for both key words <u>and</u> the human visitor who is looking for something interesting to read.

Make extensive use of links. Text links, otherwise known as anchor text, are the words you usually see underlined and highlighted in a body of text, serving as a link to some other content on the site, such as library items or other internal pages. You get extra points from search engines if your anchor text matches your key phrases.

Play Nice and Share the 'Link Love'. It is very important for your website that you make those linking connections. Most of the attorneys I talk to don't want to link from their website to other attorneys. This apprehensiveness is one of the biggest and most common mistake law firm websites make. Don't be afraid to ask other noncompetitive sites to link to your site. Search engines will reward you for it. The goal of search engine algorithms is to determine relevancy and value. The prevailing theory is that search engines will assume your site has more value and relevancy if other sites link to yours, so go out there and make some friends! When linking to your site, link from a key phrase, not your firm name. Instead of linking from "Smith & Smith PLLC," link from "[insert a keyword phrase you want to optimize for]." Search engines will reward you.

> *Note from Ben: Don't be a wimp. Work out reciprocal links with your competition, too. The upside effect from linking with other powerful sites can far outweigh the "loss" of a visitor. Hey, the consumer is going to find them anyway!*

Think of search engine optimization as a popularity contest. When you have others who like you (link to your site) your popularity improves (the more highly ranked your site becomes). Links to your site are the 3rd party vote in the popularity contest. Generally, the more people "voting" for you the better. But don't think that all links are created equal. Links from pages that have tons of outbound links are not as valuable as a link from a page that is choosy about who it links to. You want links from higher authority sites that are picky about who they will endorse. Remember this is like a popularity contest. Getting attention (a link) from the 'snobby prom queen' who doesn't like just anyone means more.

> *Note from Ben: Beware of buying links. You don't like people who pay for their friends and Search engines do not like people who pay for their links. You can find your site off of Google!*

Composing Titles and Descriptions

Most attorneys have heard of meta-keyword tags, but unless you have optimized a site before, you may not be aware that every page can have its own title tag and meta-description. This common mistake is one of the easiest to fix. It is also the most important thing you can do for SEO. No matter what else you do, unless you fix these items, nothing will work. If your site has the same title tag and meta descriptions throughout, it was designed by a rank amateur.

Use a few compelling words. Title tags are very important to search engines, and writing effective title tags and descriptions is a lot like writing headlines that use very few words. The goal is to address a problem or need and present a solution that's compelling enough to make the reader want to know more in about 25 words or less. Title tags identify the company and include the key phrase for that particular page. If you've done a good job of picking key phrases, they should be fairly easy to compose.

Include straightforward descriptions. A description should address your primary audience's need or want and your ability to help them. Here's an example:

A Google search on the key phrase "Virginia medical malpractice attorney" returns a highly ranked listing for Ben Glass Law, a Fairfax Virginia personal injury attorney. The firm's home page title tag is "Fairfax, Virginia-Best Personal Injury Car Accident Attorney Website" The page description is:

> *Free Consumer Books on Virginia Personal Injury and car accident claims are available to Virginia residents before you talk to the insurance adjuster, hire an attorney or sign any forms. These popular books are written by a nationally recognized, board certified personal injury attorney and clearly explain both the Virginia personal injury claims process and the personal injury attorney hiring process. Virginia accident and malpractice victims are beginning to realize that it's ridiculous to think that insurance companies, especially in tough economic times, are going to treat you fairly on their own. Virginia consumers also have come to understand that most lawyer advertising is bad for consumers. Bad, because most lawyer ads don't provide any really USEFUL information.*

Nothing fancy, but highly effective.

Never Miss an Opportunity to Optimize

Search engine crawlers may not read text in graphics, but they certainly read text in documents, so take advantage of all your site content by optimizing your online library. Your library should be variety of:

- Articles
- Excerpts of the law you are specializing in
- Brochures
- Firm newsletters
- Attorney publications
- Presentations you have done in PowerPoint can be converted to Adobe PDF and therefore searchable
- Client briefs and other papers describing a case in great detail. This is a great method to capture those obscure injury cases.
- Press releases

Note from Ben: Want free key word rich content? Full text court opinions can be uploaded to your site. They are in the public domain. They are available at your state court website and through Pacer. The best strategy is for you to write a "press release" comment on the case and attach the press release to the front of the court opinion before uploading. Presto! Pages and pages of free relevant content.

All these things and more can be put on your site. If you can't add or update your website on a daily bases—in real-time—then you need to find a different web developer.

Another great web marketing tool is to offer to write articles for e-zines or other publications, sprinkle your key phrases throughout the article, and, when it's published, link to it from your site. Not only will you give yourself two chances for high rankings—their e-print and yours—but you'll also create a content link that search engines love, while positioning yourself as a published author on a subject of the kind of cases you want (your practice areas).

Marketing brochures tend to be a longer, more detailed version of website content, and thus any key phrases you are optimizing on your site should easily work into brochure copy. The same goes for papers, presentations and other collateral material that may be downloaded from your site.

Press releases are a little different. Since they are supposed to present hard news, it's best to avoid marketing-speak and pay careful attention to how they are optimized. Reporters and editors are wise to the ways of public relations practitioners, so avoid optimizing too heavily for news engines at the expense of losing the interest of these very important human readers.

Pick one or two key phrases that can fit with the news angle of the story, and use them in the headline and subhead. You can include a subhead in the body copy and use a key phrase there if your release is more than a few paragraphs. Use a key phrase twice in the first paragraph of the release if possible, and then one or two other times throughout the rest of copy, depending on the overall length of the release.

• •

Ben's Bonus Success Tip #12

How can you be the "tollbooth" through which all requests for legal services flows in our community? This is the question that you must always be thinking about. Is everything I do helping to cement that position as "wise man/woman at the top of the mountain?"

• •

Every press release should include a company bio, the "About—insert your company name here—" paragraph located at the end of the release. If you can include a key phrase in the title, such as "About Smith & Smith PLLC, Florida Injury Attorneys," then by all means do so, but be careful not to use obvious marketing copy in what is **supposed to be a news release**.

Step 3: They're on Your Site. Now What?

If **Step 1** incorporates elements of market research (know your client) and **Step 2** requires understanding the preferences and nuances of search engines, then **Step 3** is a throwback to the skills and talents of a good copywriter. Good copy is art. Copywriters know how to connect with readers—make them smile, bring them to tears, sometimes even make them mad. But they always make them *feel*, and thus propel them to act. The main difference with writing for the web is that the copywriter has to be cognizant of (and adhere to) the requirements of search engines. Here are some of the key things to keep in mind when writing persuasive web copy.

Navigation for All Kinds. Always remember that prospects make quick categorization decisions. They want to know if you can help them. They want you to relate to them as a human being first, lawyer second. People are too impatient to take the time to figure out what you do on their own. You got about 15 to 30 seconds to capture their attention.

It should be "about them," not "about us." Attorney websites would be far more effective if they were mostly about what prospective clients really care about—and it's usually themselves and what they are going through. Take a look at your current website. Does its content discuss the issues the prospect might be having? Is it written compassionately? Does it demonstrate that you know your audience, what their needs are, and how your legal services will benefit them? Does it show them how they can help themselves (when appropriate)? Or, is it mostly about you or your firm? Give your copy the pronoun test. Do you see mostly "us, our, and we" or "you and yours"? Once you finish describing your firm, the copy should address "you"—your clients.

Make sure the majority of your site's content is designed to give your prospects and clients the information they really want—how your firm and using your legal services will benefit them.

Say it first quickly. Most prospective clients are on the hunt and want to find an attorney quickly. They have a problem and are looking for legal help. Think of what you say first as the "headline" for the rest of your site. Make sure it is catchy. Don't waste it on a welcome message: "Welcome to the Website of Smith & Smith."

Don't overdo the jargon. It is especially hard to resist in jargon-laden industries like law, insurance or medical. But overuse of jargon can be deadly. Most lawyer websites seem to be written for other lawyers, not for prospective clients searching for help. To stand out you have to be different.

The following is from a business's website:

> *[Company's] imaging solutions combine easy-to-use and completely configurable software with state-of-the-art hardware to manage hard-copy documents and images in digital form.*

In addition to being too wordy and packed with throw-away words, this copy doesn't mention the prospect's needs or involvement with the product, not to mention a benefit. A more effective way of saying the same thing is as follows:

> *We provide imaging hardware and software that you can customize to manage all your paper and digital documents. This frees you to do other, less labor-intensive and more important tasks.*

Give them the opportunity to respond. Each page of your website should be focused on delivering a message that is so powerful and meaningful to your target audience that it ultimately moves them to action, whether that be ordering a FREE report, signing up for your newsletter, downloading materials, or requesting a consultation with your firm. That doesn't mean that each page should have such an offer, but each page should tell a story (or part of a story) that contributes to that action. And while offers need not be placed on every page, your navigation should be such that visitors can easily take action in one or two clicks.

As a matter of fact, you should continually test calls to action to see which words elicit the best response from your particular customers. If the only web form on your site is a "contact us" or "free case evaluation" form you are not maximizing the power of your site.

"Please sign up for our newsletter" may work with some people (and that's what most websites say), but others will respond more favorably to an offer such as "Get the Top 12 Things That Car Accident Insurance Companies Do Not Want You To Know." You want to be different. You want to create many ways for web visitors to start the conversation with you.

How you elicit responses is also important. For example, if you want someone to enter an email address, you might include a statement like: "We respect your privacy…" or some other type of "anti-spam" message just below the dialog box.

Go with the flow. After you've developed your copy, give some thought to whether it flows effectively. Where are you going to put it on your website? To make it work the best for SEO, you should "link" from one of your practice area pages. Make sure that similar content are grouped together. Do messages build on one another to a logical conclusion? That conclusion is always to contact you in one way or another.

Did you start with the most important information and tie in details as you went along? Did you close effectively by giving a call to action and directions for next steps? To test how content flows, read it out loud. If it feels choppy or disconnected, edit the content to flow more smoothly.

More and more people rely heavily on the web for legal help and information. One reason is that unlike any other communications channel, the Web gives us an opportunity to educate ourselves and to do side-by-side comparisons of companies, products and services quickly and without ever leaving our chair. Organic search, via search engines like Google and Yahoo, is still the largest driver of Web traffic.

To make sure you get your fair share of that traffic, carefully choose the right keywords that represent what kind of cases you want. Then integrate those keywords throughout your site according to the guidelines I have presented. Finally, make sure you have a good copywriter who can make the keywords come alive and craft them into a compelling, creative and emotional sales case for your legal services.

> *Note from Ben: Make a note to visit the FosterWebMarketing site and <u>study</u> the portfolio of clients. Check out how their sites are laid out; what the calls to action are and how video is being used. DON'T DARE, however, copy these sites for your own use. They are the intellectual property of the owners. This tip is given to inspire.*

About the Author:

Tom Foster is the CEO of Foster Web Marketing (FWM), a web marketing and development company that helps affluent professionals, like lawyers, market themselves online. Foster Web Marketing provides numerous services, including web marketing, web design, SEO, social media marketing and online video. Visit FosterWebMarketing.com for a ton of free information that will help you communicate better with <u>your</u> webmaster.

Chapter 18

BLOGGING AS A SPECIFIC
INTERNET MARKETING TOOL
By: Tom Foster

Blogging as a form of Internet media began as a way to add fresh new content to a "mini website" in the days before good content management systems existed. Today, blogs proliferate and there are many resources, including free resources, for getting a blog up and running.

A blog is certainly no substitute for a robust, deep, multipage and multimedia website but blogs can be an essential additional tool.

The strategy is this: Develop a robust primary website for your law firm or practice niche. Then, go out and develop additional websites in the form of blogs whose purpose is twofold: (1) to help you dominate the first page of Google by having the blogs themselves position well in Google and (2) having the blogs act as feeders of traffic back to your main website.

Blogs are useful because a content management system is typically "built-in" to the blog engine. Therefore it is relatively easy, once the blog is set up, to add content. The principles of marketing remain the same: the purpose of a blog is to lead the viewer to identify themselves to you by "raising their hand" to either request your information package or to tell you about their case.

Why Blogging Generates Traffic

The best blogs are actually set up to create traffic flow much faster than websites. Smart blogging is better than hard blogging. In other words, taking advantage of the way search engines work is a much more efficient way of using your blog to attract potential clients. Simply starting a generic blog and putting paragraph upon paragraph of content is not the best way to go about it.

Here are some of the ways that your blog software should be set-up to attract both web traffic and potential clients:

Structuring of Content: Your software should allow you to categorize what you choose to blog about. For instance, if you blog about car accident law, you have a category to put it into. If you blog about medical malpractice, you have a category to put it into. If you blog about slip and falls, you have a category to put that into. Your software should allow you to very easily create categories as you need them.

Easy URL's: URL's are an incredibly important part of how search engines zero in on what the user is looking for. Rather than have a URL that is loaded with numbers or code or things that have nothing to do with either your practice or the subject on which you were blogging, your blog URLs should be a simply distilled, one term description of exactly what you blogged about. That is, each individual blog post that you put up should have its own, key word rich, URL. In other words, your blogging software should allow you to manipulate the URL for that particular blog and not just randomly assign something like www.BensBlog.com/page1.htm.

Note from Ben: If you do practice in multiple practice areas, the best strategy is to have a separate blog for each practice area. Yes, this is more work, but more work= more success. Some examples worth serious study are:

FloridaChildInjuryLawBlog.com
NYMedicalMalpracticeBlog.com
CaliforniaInjuryBlog.com
NewYorkFranchiseLaw.com
VirginiaMalpracticeNews.com
BeforeYouTalkToTheAdjuster.com

Easy Internal Linking: Placing links to other parts of your site is incredibly good for generating search engine traffic to your site, and our blog software makes it incredibly easy to do just that. If you wrote a blog article that is a continuation of an earlier article or references something on your website, creating a link to that page is as simple as cutting and pasting an address right out of the browser. There is no need to learn any code.

Fresh Content: Search engines reward fresh content. Blogs are a simple way to constantly update your site and to give the search engines new material to work with and index. The challenge of course, is finding the time to do it all. See Ben's "Strategies for Blogging" at the end of this chapter.

• •

Ben's Bonus Success Tip #13

It's very hard to market without spending any money, so the issue becomes, how will I spend my next marketing dollar? It's a resource allocation issue.

• •

Active Feedback: Blogs have a comment option, so you can give your readers an opportunity to offer you feedback as soon as they read what you have written. You should also consider that the comments can also be used to generate more traffic. These comments are, after all, simply more text that can be loaded with keywords and key phrases. The beauty of it is that you don't even have to write it.

Note from Ben: Done well, your blog should attract lots of traffic: With traffic comes negative comments. Delete comments that are obscene or defamatory but embrace comments critical of the positions you take. Encourage the debate! Defend your position! Educate people! You should welcome the traffic that controversy generates.

Shockingly, most lawyers are way too timid about taking a position and generating controversy!

Ben's Strategy For Blogging

1. Scan today's headlines, both legal and general, for topics of interest. Think: Where can I take a stand on one side of a hot issue? Is there a way that I can take a stand that is "non obvious" or even directly in opposition to the majority. Don't be afraid to be controversial.
2. Create an article about the news at your main website. This article will be approximately 300-500 words.
3. Use your blogs to create "doorways" to that article. In other words, use creative and interesting headlines in your blog articles to arouse curiosity to get people to look at your blogs. At your blog, "Teaser Copy" now leads them to a link that drives them back to your main website.
4. Invite people to participate. Ask them: "What do you think?"

5. You can use virtual assistants to help you keep an eye out for "blog fodder." You want to develop the habit of seeing everything in your world as a potential website or blog article to comment on.

(You can see how I took a position that was directly opposed to my state Trial Lawyer association by going to Google and searching for "Payee Notification Ben Glass")

Here are a Few of My Blogs
BeforeYouTalkToTheAdjuster.com
VirginiaMalpracticeNews.com

When a Consumer is Searching on the Internet

- You need to be found.

- You need to grab their attention once you are found.

- Your headline must entice them to read.

- Video reinforces your unique message and starts to build trust.

- You must make an outrageous, irresistible offer that gets them to trade their name and email.

- You make a next offer that says "I've got more" and gets them to qualify themselves and trade more complete contact information.

- You start an effective, interesting campaign that lets them decide that you are the wise man/woman at the top of the mountain.

- You add them to your newsletter database.

Chapter 19
USING ONLINE VIDEO TO GENERATE CALLS

Note from Ben: The following chapter is from the book, *How Smart Lawyers are Using Video on the Web to Get More Cases Without Breaking the Bank (Available at Amazon.com)* by Tom Foster and Gerry Oginski, Esq.

Have you noticed how many lawyers are putting video on their websites? Have you seen law firm videos on YouTube? Have you seen the statistics of people who search for an attorney online? Have you recognized the potential that online video has for you and your law firm?

Online lawyer videos are becoming the gold-standard in establishing your presence on the web. Why? Most viewers want to get to know a lawyer before calling. Video allows viewers to see, hear and decide for themselves whether they like you. Lawyers who fail to recognize the potential for marketing themselves with online video lose the ability to get new clients with this innovative tool. Lawyers who fail to recognize the benefits of attorney video lose the chance to have hundreds and thousands of viewers get to know them, without paying one dime more if 1,000 people watch their videos or if 10,000 people watch their videos. Lawyers who fail to recognize how powerful online videos have become are practicing law in the Stone Age.

One of Gerry's own videos, called, "Questions Never to Ask at a Deposition," has been viewed over 16,000 times as of this writing!

Most lawyers fail to see the incredible reach that an attorney video can have. Technolawyer.com editor Neil Squillante had this to say when comparing one of Gerry's videos to another lawyer's video: "Winner? Oginski by director's verdict!"

Another benefit to getting in on the ground floor with online video is better positioning in the video search engine results and improved website ranking on Google.

We know many lawyers who are frustrated and unhappy with their websites and the lack of calls generated by their sites. Many lawyers believe that by putting up a fancy looking website and spending $10,000 to $25,000 for a website with flash animation and cool looking pictures, they will get potential visitors to call. Guess again. Those lawyers who have been "encouraged" to part with their hard-earned dollars for these fancy websites have broken the cardinal rule of advertising.

What rule is that? (Answer: it's not about you!)

Lawyer videos are important when it comes to advertising, improving your search engine ranking and setting yourself apart from competitors, but what are some of the other benefits? Keep reading and you will find out!

1. Viewers get to see you.

Think about why you watch TV. You like to see action. You like to observe. While articles are always good, they simply do not have the same effect as a personal video that viewers can watch to decide for themselves whether you are the attorney they should call.

An educational video will distinguish you from all of your competitors. Guaranteed. They are too busy talking about themselves.

2. Viewers get to hear you.

A potential client who sees you and hears you starts to become familiar with you. It's the same reaction people get when they see a celebrity or TV personality when walking down the street. They feel as if they already know her. They've watched her on TV. They've "seen" her while in their homes and bedrooms watching TV. Now when they see that individual in person, they think they already know her.

> *Note from Gerry: This happened to me recently when I attended a Great Legal Marketing Seminar in Virginia, run by Ben Glass and my friend and co-writer Tom Foster. People who had seen my videos came up to me, introduced themselves, and said, "I feel like I already know you." That's what you want to happen with a potential client!*

3. Familiarity breeds trust.

With your educational video tips, what you strive for is what we are describing. A website viewer who is already familiar with you, your style, your mannerisms, will, all other things being equal, want to call you instead of a faceless law firm.

4. Viewers get to see how confident you are.

There are some things text cannot convey. Portraying confidence is one of them. Unless you have client testimonials describing in detail how confident you are, there is simply no better way for a viewer to see your expertise in action, short of coming into your office for an appointment.

5. Viewers learn about how you can help them.

Keep in mind that website viewers want to learn how you can help them. They really do not want to know how great you think you are. So, give the viewer what he wants: an educational video that teaches the process of how lawsuits work. Nobody teaches this information. Guess what—it's not a secret. However, most lawyers want potential clients in their offices before telling him or her all the "secrets" of how lawsuits work.

The common thinking is that the way to get the client to sign up with you is to show how knowledgeable and experienced you are. OK, that's fair. However, the online viewer looking for a lawyer will go elsewhere if you cannot distinguish yourself from your competition *right now.*

6. Video is much more compelling than text.

Here's the problem: everyone has basically the same credentials. The practicing lawyers all went to law school. They all passed the bar exam. In New York, they all passed the character and fitness committee. Every law firm has a website. Every firm has photos on it. So how are you different?

The key to online video is to get in on the ground floor now, because the longer you wait to do videos, the longer it will take you to overcome your competitors who have learned how to do videos effectively. Have you created your attorney videos yet? If not, what are you waiting for?

Note from Ben: Don't get suckered into paying tens of thousands of dollars for Hollywood—level video productions. It is not necessary. Many members of Great Legal Marketing have travelled to the Fairfax Video Studio (FairfaxVideoStudio.com) for very high quality videos at a reasonable price. Others, including Gerry, have shot highly effective videos at their offices or on a back porch.

You can see hundreds of videos that I have created at LegalAcademyVideos.com. Videos there include those produced in a studio, at the office, via PowerPoint and in the backyard.

About the Author:

Gerry Oginski is a New York lawyer who has been in practice for twenty years and has been a solo practitioner since 2002. He has created more than 100 informational online videos for his medical malpractice and personal injury practice. Realizing that most video producers don't have a deep understanding of the practice of law and what potential clients look for, Gerry launched The Lawyers' Video Studio, which provides free tutorials and video production services.

**Want to See Hundreds of Examples of
Law Firm Informational Videos?**

www.LegalAcademyVideos.com

Secrets to Creating MASSIVE VIDEO CONTENT Quickly & Easily

- State and answer 10 Frequently Asked Questions.

- State and answer 10 "Should Ask" Questions.

- Give 10 Tips for Handling Your Own Personal Injury Case

- Describe 10 steps in the process of this type of case/litigation.

- Describe 10 Tips for Finding the Right Lawyer for Your Case.

- For each of the 50 topics, shoot a "regular" short video in studio or with a flip camera.

- For each of the 50 topics, create a short (3-5 frame) PowerPoint® presentation and then do a voice-over and turn the PowerPoint into a video file.

- For each PowerPoint®, take the same 3-5 frame "presentation" and record a "live intro." For example: *Hi, this is Ben Glass with another quick tip on..."* This will give you another unique video.

- For each of the above PowerPoint® "shows", you can create a "geo-specific" presentation, optimized for a city or location.

Chapter 20

GETTING YOUR BOOK WRITTEN

By: Tom Costello, Word Association Publishers

Writing your own book may seem like a daunting task, but it really is very achievable and can be immensely helpful for your practice. You must first come to understand a few common roadblocks for writers and the easy ways to bypass them. Then, it is helpful to realize the reasons you have for writing this book and your expectations for it after publication. With these points in mind, you are sure to succeed in your efforts to be a published author.

Your own book can do wonders for your credibility and respectability in your field and can increase your clientele flow by reminding potential clients of your expertise in this certain field. A book is a valuable investment because it allows yourself to show off your depth as a lawyer and as an individual that a client is willing to trust. Writing a book on your specific area of practice establishes you as an expert in the field. When members of the media reference you, they are able to cite you as the author of your book which gives you additional clout. Possibly the most important benefit of writing a book is that it allows you to give it to clients and potential clients to keep, so that they will remember you as an expert in the field.

The first step to writing a book is to not think of it as a book at all. You want to start with a series of frequently asked questions about your area of specialty. If you think your field is too broad, find one aspect that you spend a lot of time on or particularly enjoy and focus on this smaller aspect. Then set aside 45 to 90 minutes a day to write. I would recommend this amount of time, because it will allow your ideas time to mature as well as keeping you focused. During the rest of your day, carry a notepad or recorder around with you so that you can jot down or record ideas as they come. When you begin a writing period, read aloud at least two pages of what you had written to jump start your thoughts. Before you put aside your writing for the day be sure to know where you will begin the next day to help avoid writer's block. These tips should help your writing flow.

Don't try to write like someone you're not. People are most apt to appreciate writing that sounds like its coming from a real person, so write like you speak. One of the best ways to write is to pretend you're talking to one other person sitting across the table from you. Don't write a book as if you're talking to the country or to the stadium or to a whole group of people. Address one person and if you do that well enough, everyone who's reading it will understand that it's for them. Some people find it easiest to dictate their writing in order to achieve this. Either way, be sure to let your personality shine through in your writing.

When you begin, don't concern yourself about the length. Your book will be the length that it needs to be. Most successful self-published books are less than 100 pages! Business and professional people don't have time to read 250 to 500 pages, so don't waste your time and effort on this extra information. Make your writing worth the reader's time, so it is best if your book is reader friendly. Many people fear that their writing is not good enough to write a book. Your book does not have to be an extraordinary work of art. It just needs to be competent, acceptable writing that will work well for your practice.

At Word Association, we help people like you publish their own books by providing a variety of services in one place with quick results. After you send us a manuscript, we will read through it and then send you a publishing proposal which itemizes all the services that we could offer you as a writer and a potential author. These services include marketing, editing, and cover design of which you may choose to use all or none. We offer both hardback and paperback bindings, but I am biased towards soft cover books. Trade paperback books are slightly larger format paperbacks that have sturdy soft covers that command the respect of a hardback book without the extra cost. But you must be willing to spend a couple thousand dollars to make a book that you will be proud of. If you want to have a decent book, one that reads well, that is edited and well designed, plan on spending a couple thousand dollars. That is not to say that it can't be done for less, but you pay for what you get. We provide all of our books with an ISBN, an International Standard Book Number. The ISBN is a universal number that only your book has and using that number, anyone in the world can order that book. So without that number your book is simply not in the book industry database and will never be found. We also get the Library of Congress number for most books, which is an ordering number that gives your book some more respectability, but requires that your book be at least 42 pages long.

Since many people judge a book by its cover, and back cover, these aspects of your book are very important. We help you come up with a nice design based on any ideas or guidelines that you provide. The back cover is almost as essential as the front, because it is usually the second place potential readers turn. We ask authors to write a draft of the back cover copy and then we help fine-tune it so that it becomes as polished and as much of a hook as we can make it. I also recommend that authors include a picture of themselves either on the back cover or on the last page of the book. Reading and writing are very personal things and just getting a picture of the author in a reader's head somehow makes them more comfortable with the author.

Aggressive business and professional people are always looking for an angle, a marketing tool that's completely original, one that will leave the competition wondering what hit them and what I want to suggest is that we all have this potential tool in our possession. It takes work. It will take some time, but the tool is a book and you are its author, the business person, a professional. The psychic distance between a published book and any other document is that they are fine way to get the word out, but they are limited. They can only go so far. They're sound bites beside a full range of possibilities offered by a book. Writing a book will do wonders for your business or practice and will be well worth all the effort you put into it.

About the Author:

Tom Costello, Ph.D. is the publisher and editor at Word Association. His company offers writers a way to publish their book with all of the advantages of self-publishing and none of the negatives of a vanity press. Word Association is a one-stop shop that provides editing and proofreading, manuscript consultation, co-writing, ghostwriting, manuscript preparation (typesetting or page formatting), cover and interior design, credentials (ISBN, Library of Congress Number, copyright), printing and binding, promotion and marketing, and distribution and fulfillment.

● ●

Ben's Bonus Success Tip #14

As we see the proliferation of lawyer rating sites on the Internet, everything from Avvo to real nut ball sites that allow anyone to post defamatory messages about you, it becomes really important that you have a raving fan base to protect you and come to your "defense." Assuming that you've got people who love you and who appreciate you, you say to them, "Oh, there's a nut ball comment over at this website. If you don't mind and you've got a different opinion, would you go visit the website?"

● ●

Chapter 21

THE "SHOCK AND AWE PACKAGE"
(When the potential client decides that you are the wise man/woman at the top of the mountain.)

What happens when your marketing has achieved one of its main goals: the request for information from you? Most lawyers send a letter. You shock them and create massive interest in you!

The potential client who has indicated that they want to hear from you because you made in "irresistible offer" in your marketing package should receive a package full of great information that can include:

1. The book they requested
2. A book that educates the prospect on how to find the right lawyer for their case.
3. An audio CD in which you speak to the prospective client, either "solo" or through an interview format.
4. A DVD of a television show where you are interviewed.
5. A "brag book" of testimonials
6. Reprints of articles you have written or that have been written about you.
7. "Accident kits" for their car.
8. Past issues of your newsletter.
9. Press releases your firm has issued and has anything else you can think of that would be ethical, interesting, and informative.

This package can be in a big box or a large envelope. Yes, you will spend some money. No, they won't read or listen to <u>all</u> of it. Remember some people learn by reading, some by listening and others by watching. You can't know which will work best for your next client so you sent it all.

Expensive and time consuming to mail such a large package? Maybe. But as an attorney, the transaction value of each case is large. Don't be cheap about this.

Note from Ben: When you join our Great Legal Marketing coaching program I'll send you our "shock and awe" package that we use for personal injury cases, for free. This is a special offer only for people who have registered this book (RegisterTheBook.com) and you must write, "send me the P.I. Shock and Awe Package" on your coaching application.

Our BenGlassLaw Shock and Awe Package is Mailed in This Envelope

Chapter 22
LAWYERS AND SOCIAL MEDIA

What Do We Do With Facebook, LinkedIn and Whatever Else Might Be the Flavor of Next Week?

By: Charley Mann, Great Legal Marketing

Ignoring social media and social networking these days is the equivalent of an ostrich shoving its head in the sand. Just because you choose not to see something going on around you, it doesn't mean it's not there and happening. The online world is constantly "on" and you can't turn it "off" by turning your back on it.

Social media's effect is compounded by its rapid adoption in groups well outside of your standard college-agers. Many predicted at first that it would be a youth-only tool. That was the case originally; however, more people are signing up for services such as Facebook, Twitter and LinkedIn every day. The age gap is continuing to thin as online networkers grow in age and encourage everyone around them to join in on the fun. Thousands of new people in the United States sign up every day, from age 13 to 99+. They work in all fields, they represent all religions, they have all kinds of income levels, they come from all regions, and they connect with people throughout their communities.

Ultimately, using the "my consumer base isn't on Facebook" argument is a waste of breath and a potentially dangerous attitude to take in today's hyper-competitive online marketing world. Of course, arguing that somehow Facebook is "beneath the dignity" of lawyers is also old-school. The train is leaving the station—get on it.

Of course, social media for some still remains a foreign concept. Essentially, social media is an online outlet for individuals and businesses to express themselves and communicate with others in the community. There are hundreds of sites that fall under the category of "social media," though smart marketing is all about finding the most effective arenas, so it is best to focus on the following: Facebook, Twitter, LinkedIn, and YouTube (with the eventual inclusion of Google+). You can also include blogs under the umbrella term of social media, as well.

Social networking, on the other hand, is the way that many people utilize social media services. If social media is the way in which people broadcast messages, then social networking is the communicating and connecting that occurs within those channels. You use social media to increase your social networking capabilities.

These media and rapid-fire forms of communication have altered the way people interact on a fundamental level. Sharing what you read, watch and listen to have become standard practice. On the same level, people share general experiences. These include trips they've taken, foods they've eaten, and companies with which they do business.

With all of that information, take a quick step back to build the marketing picture that Ben Glass has already drawn for you:

- **Referrals:** As you build a client base, you are also building your own little army that can recruit more troops for you (assuming you did a good job and they like you). Referred clients tend to be great clients. Social media is a vehicle that they can use to evangelize for you. You need to make that easy for them.
- **Testimonials:** If you can't get a one-to-one referral, then the next best thing is getting a testimonial to share with any potential clients. Make sure to get permission from the person to share it in all of your media, including online and offline publications.
- **Being Found:** When people look for a lawyer, doctor, chiropractor, etc., they like to shop around. What is the first venue most potential clients choose to fulfill their needs? You'd better believe it is the Internet. Remember, Google wants to return the most relevant results.

Sometimes the most relevant result that Google returns is a posting from social media.

- **Information:** Potential clients like to know more about the choice they are about to make. In today's world of Lawyers.com® and LegalZoom®, you need ways to deliver information that is useful to consumers before they wander off to other places to get their questions answered.

- **Interactions:** The one-on-one interactions that you have with potential clients are integral to strengthening the troops of your army.

- **Reputation:** Having control over your reputation can never be ignored. No one wants to hire a lawyer that people think is a sleazy ne'er-do-well. An army of devotees can help drown out that pesky "negative comment" that one disgruntled person posts about your firm.

Each one of these categories is greatly enhanced by a strong presence on social media sites. The upkeep of these sites and the proper use of social networking strategies can be the final key to stepping up the profit level of your business.

The embracing of social media by every generation has made it a valuable source for **referrals**. A law firm's Facebook page or Twitter handle can be shared easily from one person to another, but only if you're playing in that space. Likewise, the sharing of YouTube videos is an extremely popular method of communication.

Quick tip: Make sure all of your social media profiles have easy-to-use, recognizable calls-to-action for effective online **referrals** that have strong conversion rates.

Testimonials can be shared through so many social media sites. Something as simple as a status update on Facebook saying thank you to the person who shared the **testimonial** with a short quote is a great way to offer rolling updates on how satisfied your customers are with your service. Plus, you are likely to get some kind of interaction from the person who offered the **testimonial** that will be noticed by his or her friends.

Quick tip: Video testimonials are incredibly powerful.

The age of social search is here. **Being found** online these days requires a stellar combination of search engine optimization and social media enhancement. All of the major search engines are building in algorithms that take social media into account. This means that **being found** will soon *require* a social presence. Plus, for many businesses, their Facebook/LinkedIn page, Twitter account,

YouTube channel and other online profiles rank highly and allow them to dominate the first page of Google.

Quick tip: Interaction with your social media sites is even more important that your number of "fans," so make sure to produce high-quality content.

The distribution of free **information** is the best way to build your reputation as an expert in your profession. By using social media, you create a two-fold method to serve potential clients better. One, you create a broadcast system for your **information** that makes it more easily found by those in need. Two, the same broadcast system is able to put your **information** in the hands of merely curious consumers who may need your help in the future.

Quick tip: Make sure that you are tracking the effectiveness of these distribution systems.

People communicate in many different ways these days, which means that you need to be able to facilitate **interactions** in many arenas. Social media allows you to respond rapidly to people without crowding your email inbox. Plus, these **interactions** are public and can be found by others who may have similar questions. As you build your online army, you will see people have positive **interactions** with others about you online, which can, again, be seen by everyone. Plus, you build a fort around yourself that your army defends if you are attacked online.

Quick tip: People generally expect a response within 12-24 hours, if not sooner, but be careful about wasting time on social media by checking it too often.

So many service professionals take pride in their **reputations**, yet they fail to parry attacks from online sources. The fact is that as more conversations move online, the more likely it is that your business will be brought up at some point. If you don't get in on the game, people can still trash your **reputation** without your ever having a chance to respond.

Quick tip: One of the most effective ways to turn around a person's opinion about you is to address it head on and rectify the situation in a positive fashion.

Most social media sites are free and can be learned through experimentation with the features. They can add a whole new layer to your marketing strategies and are an excellent complement to initiatives you already have in place. The fact is that if you don't act on it and build a full online presence that includes social media, someone else in your area will, leaving you to wonder where the clients went.

About the Author:

Charley Mann is the Business Development Specialist for Great Legal Marketing and BenGlassLaw. He has done individual consultations with attorneys across the nation for social media presence development. Additionally, Charley produces and hosts the weekly Make Marketing Happen podcast, which can be found on iTunes by typing in "Make Marketing Happen" in the iTunes search bar.

Chapter 23

TRACKING RESULTS—AN OVERVIEW

Tracking the results of your marketing efforts is important. Knowing where your cases are coming from helps you decide where to spend your next dollar or next hour of marketing. It is important to be as precise as you can but in today's multimedia marketing world I will be the first to admit that I sometimes sacrifice precision for "getting more things done." That being said, it is important to know when the marketing vulture comes around to sell you more ad space in their media whether or not what you spent last year in that media was productive. We determine our marketing "budget" not by some formula that is a percentage of income or net or gross but by understanding what the return on investment is.

As usual, I'm going to suggest a slightly different approach to gauging return on investment. Remember first of all that our marketing is twofold. We hope to attract today's case, but we also hope to attract tomorrow's case by obtaining, today, the names and addresses of people who find us interesting. They may not have any case today or they may not have a case that we want. Building that database of people who do find us interesting and with whom we will be "top of mind" later is vital. Remember, the database is your most important asset.

Therefore, if we do some form of advertising and we can at least break even in terms of the cases we actually get from it today, but we add names to our database, all of whom have some value to us later on, then we are "net positive" on the marketing piece. Now the only question is whether there is a type of advertisement or media where we can get a better ROI. Let me also suggest here that "1" is a very dangerous number. We do not want to rely on "1" of anything to market our practices. It would be very dangerous indeed to rely solely on referrals or solely on the Yellow Pages or solely on the Internet because any one of these could go away in the future. Any one of these advertising methods could be so drastically changed that they have effectively gone away in the future. (Go back and re-read the last chapter—will people search for lawyers tomorrow the same way they are searching today?) Therefore what we are looking to achieve is a portfolio of marketing messages and media that allows us to produce great results overall.

Here are some ways that you can use to track marketing results:

1. **Special tracking telephone numbers**. The Yellow Page reps sold these for years but today there are any number of firms from which you can obtain local or toll free numbers. There is a danger in only looking at the number of calls that come through a particular number, however. With so many people using cell phones and simply hitting "redial" that special number you bought and paid for may be used over and over by the same client or prospect. Therefore, if you are using tracking numbers it is vital that you go deeper. As you'll see in the next chapter, Richard Seppala (The ROI Guy) allows you to go much deeper than merely tracking the number of calls through a particular number.

2. **Tracking URLs**. I personally own over 300 URLs. (I buy them through GoDaddy.com, but there are many other sources.) This way, when we run any marketing piece we can create a specialized "landing page" that is affiliated with a specific easy to read and easy to spell URL. Simply put, we have the ability to know when a consumer fills out a webform exactly which ad they saw or heard before going on the web.

3. **Tracking web forms**. When you get a web contact through your website today, do you know which page they came through? (Of course you might if you only have one web form and that's on the front page of your site). You should have web forms soliciting contact information or making an offer for your books or information packages throughout your website. Each web form can be specifically tracked so that you know exactly what page the visitor came through. This tracking can be totally automated with InfusionSoft.

4. **Ask the potential client**. Of course this method is the least precise. We've had clients tell us they found us in the Yellow Pages even though we haven't been there in years.

The point is that when we are making a decision as to where to "go next" with our marketing we want to 1) know what is and isn't working and we want 2) diversity.

Chapter 24

CALL RECORDING AND MANAGEMENT FOR MAXIMUM ROI MARKETING

By: Richard Seppala, "The ROI Guy"

In the highly competitive legal market place law firms must manage the marketing budget more closely than in the past. In today's market more than ever, it is time to hone in on your message and do a targeted marketing campaign.

However, many attorneys fall prey to a faulty marketing model I call the **shotgun approach**. They see what other lawyers are doing and simply follow suit. If they see a competitor's full-page Yellow Pages ad, they assume this kind of marketing must be working because others are doing it, so they take out an ad as well. They may even sign a contract with a newspaper or magazine without determining whether this tactic will work for their niche. They may try all different kinds of advertising, but fail to track each individual campaign to determine what's working and what isn't.

This tactic becomes especially dangerous when small or medium business owners start trying to model their marketing after bigger players. They try to brand their name instead of doing key lead generation tactics that track and convert leads to sales. Unless you're Coca-Cola or McDonald's, you can't rely on brand name to grow your business. National branding campaigns create astronomical expenses that many smaller businesses can't support, especially now.

However, business owners can manage their marketing budget, increase market share, continue to advertise, and still get ROI—return on investment—by using a call management and recording service to track the success of each individual campaign.

How to Target Your Market with Call Measurement

Call measurement is the most important ingredient in a marketing ad or campaign. If business owners aren't using call measurement, they won't know where the business they've generated is coming from, so they have to keep spending the same amount of marketing dollars each month to continue producing acceptable levels of sales.

Call measurement is an advertising secret a lot of advertising agencies don't want you to know about because you can hold them accountable for the response rates that they recommend and sell you on.

With a call measurement system, business owners can hone in on where responses are coming from, which offers the leads are being attracted to, and what made each prospect contact them. Call measurement helps distinguish which campaigns work, and which don't work and should be discontinued. This system brings down your marketing budget and gives you a better return on investment, which at the end of the day, means more money in your pocket.

Call measurement provides business owners with unique telephone numbers, local or toll-free, to place in their marketing campaigns instead of their main office number. Because leads call a particular number to schedule an appointment, results from the individual marketing campaigns can be measured by comparing the different results from the different telephone numbers used for each campaign.

With today's technology, when an individual calls from one of those tracking numbers, it goes through a server that captures the caller's name, number, and address and some basic demographic information. Most importantly, the ad source that generated that call is also tracked. The best part is that the call goes seamlessly to the receptionist or the front desk or the sales staff of the company.

Call Recording for Business Value

Any business interested in growing to the next level, honing in on their marketing campaigns, and spending their marketing budget efficiently, can benefit from call recording. Call recording enables business owners to provide ongoing training and increase employee skills, so they can convert more callers to customers.

A lot of business owners, especially in a tight economy, believe that their marketing isn't working; so they cut their marketing budget and use the money somewhere else. Sometimes marketing efforts don't work because the company isn't tracking their marketing, as we've discussed; but most of the time it's because calls are being poorly handled.

A marketing campaign may have generated hundreds of responses, yet only a percentage of those reach the company. When the leads come in, some calls aren't handled properly. Was the phone even answered? Did the person who answered the phone try to convert the caller to a client? Did they offer the "shock and awe" package, or was it what we call a "data dump"—just giving the caller a fee or other basic information and letting them go instead of building the trust and working the relationship?

Businesses that have implemented call recording have seen performance ratios increase dramatically because employees know management might be listening. But call recording is as much a training tool as it is an accountability tool. Business owners can use these audio recordings for training purposes and to evaluate how effectively the call was handled. They can also use the calls to call create scripts for common customer questions, and to listen to how scripts actually sound when used on calls.

Where the ROI Guy Comes in

The ROI guy has saved attorneys just like you thousands, even hundreds of thousands of dollars in marketing budgets while increasing their marketing ROI. My company, Total Census Solutions, provides a true ROI for marketing and advertising campaigns by showing business owners which of their campaigns are successful and which aren't working. We give them the ammunition and reinforcement they need so they're not "fighting blind." We let them know that a campaign hasn't really provided any leads in the last two months, so they can tweak the call to action or the placement.

I know this strategy works because I saw it in action with my wife's dental practice. She came to me frustrated and said, "Richard, we spent all this money on marketing and advertising and we aren't getting any new patients." After a little bit of research, I suggested that we put a tracking number on her next direct mail campaign to see what was actually happening.

We evaluated how many leads came in from the next direct mailing, and we also evaluated how those new patients were handled when they called in. What we learned was almost devastating, but it was a savior to the business. In reality she was receiving more than one hundred new leads a month, but she wasn't even converting 10 percent of those leads.

Leads weren't converted to appointments because of poor phone techniques or poor phone training skills. Phones weren't being answered, or people were calling after hours and not leaving messages.

I helped her train her staff to handle the incoming calls and convert those callers to new appointments, and she tweaked her staffing hours to be available when the peak calls were coming in. In the first 30 days, she increased her revenue by more than $100,000 by implementing these basic systems.

The best thing about the ROI Guy system is how easy it is to use. It's as simple as calling us and saying that you want to track a marketing campaign. Within twenty-four hours, we will provide you with a unique toll-free or local phone number.

There's no hardware or software on your end. There's nothing to download. All you do is place the phone number we give you in your ad, and our system does the rest: evaluation, tracking, recording. And all our information is in real time so you can make real-time decisions. You don't have to wait thirty days to see what the results were. You'll know instantaneously with the ROI Guy system.

We don't just give you a couple of new phone numbers and some data at the end of the month. We provide you with daily, weekly, and monthly summaries to help you understand the process, and we provide coaching to help you understand the data in order to make better choices and get the most ROI out of your marketing campaigns. We help you train your employees to make the most of the results. It's a very integrated approach, and we're with you all along the way.

About the Author:

Richard Seppala, also known as "The ROI Guy ™," is constantly asking the question "What is the return on the investment you make for each of your marketing campaigns?" Seppala founded what has now become The ROI Guy in 2005 and provides advertising tracking for clients nationwide. The ROI Guy ™ Tracking System monitors the success or failure of ad campaigns, tracks marketing response rates, determines return on investment (ROI) and identifies the strengths and weaknesses of your marketing and customer service programs throughout your business lifecycle.

Critically acclaimed as "The Holy Grail of Marketing," The ROI Guy ™ Tracking System is just that, as there is no easier system that "puts the power and ease of real time results for lead generation on autopilot with all of your marketing campaigns.

To learn more about Richard Seppala, The ROI Guy™ and how you can receive the free Special Report "Your Income Explosion Guide: 7 Powerful Reasons Why Your Telephone is the Lifeblood of Your Business," visit www. YourROIGuy.com or call Toll-Free 1-800-647-1909.

Chapter 25

POWERFULLY PROFITABLE DIRECT RESPONSE RADIO ADVERTISING

By: Harmony Tenney, MBA
Direct Response Radio Advertising Consultant for Lawyers

Radio advertising is one of the most uncharted territories in the lawyer advertising world! It is rare to find an attorney who knows what works, what doesn't, and how to make radio yield a bumper crop of prospective and profitable clients year after year. Yet radio advertising is particularly gifted at targeting groups and delivering salient information. For example, it reaches 88% of persons whose household have used a personal injury attorney in the past year, and 90% of households who have used an attorney's service in the past year (www.RAB.com). Radio removes consumer objections and warms prospective clients to a state of having "heard about you"—all positive, thanks to your ads.

Direct response radio advertising is King, having succeeded its elder brother, branding. "Branding" has long been the default marketing objective—it's now a cluttered catch-all phrase. Being able to know, quickly, which ads on which stations are pulling the most requests for information is inherent to traceable, incremental return on investment. Radio has stated over and over that its intangibility is nothing to be feared (and I've personally wielded even branding ads into profitable frenzies, so I agree), but being able to put data where one's mouth is—that's priceless! Direct response radio ads elicit response from listeners—immediately.

Most lawyers utilize direct response radio ads to get book or information requests, so they can place respondents in their marketing sequence. The process is pretty simple (drive people to a website or phone number), but it takes a lot of time and footwork to pick the right station, schedule and ad.

Choose a station that reaches your target demo (men, women, affluent, multi-cultural, various age groups, etc), covers your preferred service area (can be neighborhood specific, state specific, large or small), and gives you correct frequency (number of times listeners are offered their chance to respond to your ads) from within your budget. It's important that you don't just pick the station you regularly listen to. You are NOT your client, and you can flush a lot of money away due to being egocentric.

You'll need to build a solid schedule. Radio divides each day into 4 to 5 hour segments: Morning Drive, Midday, Afternoon Drive, Evening and Overnight. You should ask what time of day the station has the most listeners in your target group (the answer is NOT always drive time). Also, check for special programming, such as a feature, or call-in shows that would be relevant to your particular practice. Then, find out what "extras" are available, such as bonus ads or web-links. Finally, ask what community events the station is involved with that mirror your various practice areas and personal charitable giving preferences. There might be a promotion catering to a particular niche in your practice (such as a sponsorship of a charity ride for motorcyclists, or giveaways of bikes to area kids).

Building a solid schedule is pretty simple-make sure you "own" one or two day parts or features weekly. If you've chosen a music station, try 2 per day for five weekdays during one 4 hour period *OR*

Three per day for at least 3 weekdays during a single 4 or 5 hr period. *THEN ADD* another set of either of the above, making 18—20 ads per week. If you're advertising on a news / talk / sports station, you'll need to make sure you have ads all but one hour of the show, daily, so that the listeners get to know you and associate your practice with the show. Make sure you're on at least two weeks per month. Decide whether you'd like to advertise the first and third weeks, or the second and fourth weeks. Later, test two weeks in a row, or advertising three weeks of the month.

If there are external factors that bear on the number of potential cases coming into your practice (such as bad weather for extra accident likelihood or first quarter seasonality of divorces) take these into account when building your schedule. You might want to add many more ads during those times, to capture a higher percentage of the available market share.

Crafting your message is important. It must be written with your objective in mind: to share how to get your book (if you have written one) and why having your book matters. Give one-way to respond-website or phone #. Air only one ad at a time—NEVER rotate more than one ad, unless you have a high frequency schedule for each one. Having two ads rotate on one schedule dilutes your frequency and wastes-literally—your money.

Voicing the ad is easy. Stations produce ads for free, and the most loyal listeners perceive the DJs as family. However, you should test to determine if an "out of the area" voice gets more response than one the loyal listeners are used to. Should you pay for an endorsement by an on-air talent? It's not usually worth it, but there are some proven ads that work well in that construct. Just realize, that even "live read" ads are scripted. Great artists can make it sound ad-libbed. As for music-it's optional—but make sure it does not overpower or take away from your message in any way. Better to go without music than chance it (don't be talked into it, either).

Don't count yourself out of promotional participation on a station. You can give a way your book, nicely packaged in a basket with a certificate for dinner for two at a nice restaurant, a car washing kit in a bucket, or even T-Shirts / tasteful imprinted promotional items. You needn't concern yourself with whomever receives the giveaway. What's important is that you just got your book mentioned to umpteen listeners who are already familiar with you—and most stations do these giveaways *gratis*. With ad prices in triple digits, *gratis* is a wonderful addition to your strategy!

You'd think that your first day on the air was the end of your work, but it's actually the culmination of the pre-work necessary to begin the profit-building momentum of your campaign. Tracking your responses is the next, and critical, step. Using your contact / database management system, note each contact received (call, email, etc) along with the date and time. Ask how the respondent heard about your practice. Note the city and state of the caller's residence (if you're advertising out of state, ask if they have recently traveled in the area you're advertising in), inquire about their three favorite radio stations (to provide future station ideas for testing and market expansion). Finally, total up how many calls were received each day, week and month-cross-referencing your responses with the days, times and weeks you advertise.

Please note, that in today's sea of information and information access, that people can look up your phone numbers, your web address, your name and practice-in any number of ways. Make sure you all the callers, web visitors and respondents how they heard about you. Your radio ads will boost any other advertising that you do, so refer back to your baseline to see the effect of your radio advertising on all the *means of contact* you have in place for your practice.

For best results from direct response radio advertising, make sure to refine the campaign over time. A word of caution here-*don't* make changes too fast, *do* confirm any hypothesis with facts, and *don't* change more than one thing as you go. If you did not get response at all after your two weeks, move all your ads to run just one or two days. Other parameters to test are the ad wording and the schedule (advertise in a different show, at a different time of day or change your station). Again, one change at a time, until you determine what message is best speaking to your prospective clients' needs, and where large pools of those hungry prospects are gathered.

Capturing more market share once you've got a good number of requests coming in is easy-you just repeat the process! Add another day part on your current station, add another station (especially one of your current respondents' favorites) or go after another niche (for example, a personal injury attorney that has successfully pulled in respondents for auto accident info can then add motorcycle, or tractor-trailer).

Whatever your practice area, for best results, make sure you begin tracking before you begin advertising. You'll then have a baseline for "what's occurring" without the direct response advertising, which will aid in your comparisons later. Additionally, you'll need to have a great offer for the listeners to respond to- a free book or a free report, a tracking mechanism that you put in place prior to the first ad's airing, a database ready to capture all the visitor vitals, and a mechanism for communicating with all respondents at least monthly. Plan all of this out in advance. Be prepared to offer a memorable experience to those newly attracted to your practice.

Beware—once you actually begin advertising, every rep in the area (TV, Radio, Outdoor Billboard, etc) will come knocking on your door or calling via phone. "Monitoring" other media is an essential part of all rep's prospecting methodology. If you have a radio-advertising consultant, you can just direct these reps there. Your consultant will be versed in the goals of your practice and will be able to judge compatibility, and if desired, a "test" campaign. Do-It-Yourself practitioners might choose to say, "we're not interested," which will save a lot of time and energy, and maintain strategic focus.

Finally, having one key person designated to oversee the campaign, either in your practice or a consultant outside of it, will allow you to keep up with the tracking, analysis of resulting data, and recommendations for next moves (testing / increasing market share).

About the Author:

Harmony Tenney is a Direct Response Radio Advertising Consultant for Lawyers. In 2006, Radio Ink Magazine recognized her as a Top Ten National Finalist for Account Executive of the Year. Before her specialization, Ms. Tenney helped small business owners in many industries achieve double digit growth through profitable radio advertising initiatives-even in flat markets. Her clients nicknamed her "The Profit Panther," and both her undergrad and graduate classmates voted her Most Likely to Appear on the Cover of Business Week. Ms. Tenney offers guaranteed and proven results from her "Powerfully Profitable, Done-for-You Radio Advertising." She also offers several Do-It-Yourself Guides for those seeking to utilize radio advertising most effectively in their marketing sequences. For a free report and audio CD "The Top Ten Things You Must Know Before Purchasing Radio Advertising," contact Harmony at: 540-255-5686, or by email: Harmony@RadioForLegal.com.

Note From Ben: When you set-up your direct response radio campaign, think carefully about three things:

1. *What is your offer? We are not running old fashioned brand building ads about your law firm. We are making an irresistible offer that compels the listener to identify themselves to us.*
2. *If your listener hears your ad while driving will they be able to remember the telephone number or URL you give them later? An easy to remember "vanity" 800 number is important, but because so many people will go on to the internet, an easy to remember, easy to spell URL is a must. Use GoDaddy or another domain purchasing site to find something like FreeAccidentBook.com or CallBenGlass.com, not OlweissLawFirm.com. Think about how your URL will sound on the radio.*
3. *Think about what will happen when they do respond. If you are driving the listener to the internet, never just use your main "front" web page of your website. Rather, create a video and put that on a specific page. The video might say something like. "Hi, this is Dan, thanks for coming here after hearing [local radio host] talk about our firm today. You've made a great decision..."*

Remember that whatever the listener does to start the process of raising their hand to ask for information, they go into your marketing sequence, get your "shock and awe" package and now ill be regularly mailed your firm newsletter.

You can listen to both of these ads (and a new one I just produced) when you get the Free CD I'll send you when you register this book (RegisterTheBook.com)

• •

Ben's Bonus Success Tip #16

Please, please, please. Before you buy any advertising, you must have a plan in place and know the answers to these questions:

1. *What happens when the advertising works and people raise their hands to say they want to talk to us?*

2. *What happens to the names of those people who contact us, but either do not have a case that we want or are not ready to hire an attorney? How will each of these groups of contacts be marketed to in the future?*

3. *How can we be sure that everyone who contacts us, no matter what media they use, their names and contact information is automatically added to our database?*

4. *What will we be saying to our mailing to good prospects that will convince them that we are the wise man/woman at the top of the mountain without using silly advertising or violating any ethical concerns?*

5. *How can we keep a prospect from searching for another lawyer in an ethical, dignified way?*

6. *How can we educate clients about the process and manage their expectations when we are marketing?*

7. *How can we stay in contact with those who have contacted us, on a monthly basis, in an interesting way, so that they next time they or someone in their circle of friends and acquaintances needs someone like us, we are "top of mind" without having spent millions of dollars on TV advertising?*

8. *How can we be the "tollbooth" through which all requests for legal services flows in our community?*

• •

Chapter 26

HOW TO MAXIMIZE YOUR TV AD BUDGET IN A VERY DIFFICULT MEDIUM

The television is becoming an increasingly difficult media for lawyers to conquer. Sure, its relatively easy to produce an ad and there are even companies that will insert your name in a "canned" ad and then tell you to run it 738 times a month to "put your name out there." There are firms that are willing to spend millions on TV advertising but there is a better and smarter way for the rest of us.

The 4 Big problems with "TV Advertising"

1. There may be more than 250 channels that people can choose to watch in your area. Where will you invest your dollar?
2. TV commercials are short. Which message are you going to convey in 30 seconds?
3. The ads "disappear" in 30 seconds, so if your prospect was heading to the refrigerator during "the commercials" you are screwed.
4. Tivo and other "commercial elimination" devices.
5. People don't sit in front of a TV, beer in hand, and say to themselves "Gee, I hope some lawyer ads are on, I was thinking about hiring one."

As you might imagine by now, the basic principles of Great Legal Marketing TV advertising are the same as with other media:

1. Study the messages of the competition.
2. Create a different message.
3. Make the ad <u>about the book,</u> not about you or your firm.
4. Use a unique URL and phone number for tracking purposes.

5. Build a specialized web "landing page" for the unique URL.
6. Have a follow-up system for any prospect who visits the URL or calls the phone number.

Sure, it's easy to <u>not</u> do these 6 steps. Go ahead. Skip them if you want, but don't complain later.

The big idea that almost all attorney marketers miss is that you have <u>two</u> major goals with your ad:

1. Get cases.
2. Build the herd.

I can guarantee you (because I've talked to many of them) that 99.9% of those firms that are spending millions of dollars to run TV ads in your area are doing <u>nothing</u> with the names of the people who call them but who have no case today!

Tips from Lawyer TV Advertising Expert Ilene Kahan.

1. Talk to a sales manager.
2. You must know how to track the lead <u>before </u>the commercial runs.
3. Get the station to work to <u>your</u> budget (not use your budget as the starting point.)
4. Don't delegate the script writing to the station!
5. Hire an expert buyer to help you. Ilene Kayhan has helped many Great Legal Marketing members place their TV Advertising. You can reach

   her directly at Ifk913@yahoo.com or at (248)-854-0908.

Chapter 27
I'M A LAWYER, NOT A CELEBRITY...OR AM I?

Note from Ben: *A time proven way to improve the marketing of any business is with the use of a celebrity. Used properly, a celebrity attracts interest, creates rapport, and lowers consumer resistance. A celebrity can help brand your firm in the minds of consumers.*

"But wait," you say. "I'm not allowed to use a celebrity in my marketing in my state." "Besides," you continue, even if I could they are really expensive."

Stop.

Who said you had to go out and find (and then rent) a celebrity? You should be the celebrity. You can be the celebrity lawyer in your niche in your geographic area (and you don't have to do anything that would embarrass your mother to be THE celebrity lawyer to your market.)

Nick Nanton is known as *the celebrity lawyer.* He has helped doctors, dentists, chiropractors and lawyers establish themselves as the trusted expert. Nick even has a 12-month program where he guarantees publicity for you on www.BenAndNick.com

I asked Nick for his top five strategies for becoming a celebrity in your area (its not as hard as you think!) Here what he had to say:

When lawyers first learn that I coach on the topic of Celebrity Branding®, many of them shut down almost instantly. It's funny, because if there was one subject most American's are obsessed with, if they would admit it (yes guys, you too!), it's celebrities. But I'm actually not talking about Paris Hilton, Britney Spears, Oprah or Dr. Phil. I coach lawyers how to charge more for the same services they are offering now, create recurring revenue streams in their practice and lock out their competitors in their practice specialty. How, you ask? Using the power of Celebrity Branding®!

Interested now?!

Celebrity Branding® is a series of strategies used to get a specific market, those who are looking for what you have to offer, to find you everywhere they turn. When executed correctly, your prospects hardly know anyone else exists, but you. It's all about finding out what your potential clients are searching for, and how they're searching for it. Next you develop specific ways for your prospect to find you and then finally, help your prospect learn more about you, your philosophy, why you're right for them, and how they can reach you.

I can do this for lawyers because I use the same strategies that big Hollywood PR agents use, to seed the media (online and offline, mass media and targeted media) with the information that I want my clients' (the lawyers who hire me), prospects and clients to know. It's one of the oldest strategies around, but it's been heavily guarded for years by Hollywood gatekeepers who want to keep the media, and the money, to themselves.

Let me show you five of my key strategies for building Celebrity status in your practice.

1. Websites

Notice I said websites, plural. Yes, one great website it a great start, but you should have multiple websites. One for your law firm, one about you personally, one with video and audio of you, one for social media connections, and the list goes on and on. Why? Because Google, except in very rare circumstances, will only show one website, one time in it's organic rankings. That means that if you only have one website, you're only going to get one listing in Google for it. If you have multiple sites, you get multiple listings in the rankings, not to mention if executed correctly, it can really help your prospects see other dimensions of your personality.

Note from Ben: Most lawyers cringe when hearing the strategy of "opening up" your personal side to the public. Get over it. Done properly, it is one of the most powerful tools you have to influence your past and current clients and your new prospects.

I won't tell you to give away your kids' cell phone numbers, and the name of your proctologist or anything. However, sharing real life stories, photos, video and info, are all great ways to break down the barriers that often stop clients from reaching out to you in the first place. Most lawyers don't have TV commercials, newsletters or anything else that has more than one dimension, which is a great point to differentiate yourself from the rest of your competition.

2. Blogs

Many of you know what a blog is, but for those who don't, it is a dedicated place for you to communicate with your clients and prospects.

A blog (short for a web log) is an online journal or diary that allows you to write and post information or ideas you feel will be of interest to your readers.

Our three principles of blogging for search engines are:

1. Write Often
2. Write Relevant
3. Write Using Key Words

What makes a good blog?

The only thing that really matters is the opinion of the audience you are trying to reach. Here are a few tips that will help you develop your blog to generate business.

1. **Know who you are writing for.** As a basic example, that hopefully won't offend anyone: If your audience is 13-year-olds, writing about retiring next year probably isn't going to get you a lot of return visitors. Writing about becoming a teenager, the best car to get when you turn 16 and how to attract the opposite sex will probably make you pretty popular.
2. **Keep it short and to the point.** Approximately 100-300 words is all most people have the time to read. Remember, in the online world, people are looking for actionable answers -- not novels (or they would go to a bookstore). So, keep your blogs short and to-the-point. Over time, you will build a great deal of credibility with your readers.
3. **Write actionable content.** "How To's" and "Top 10" lists are great. It gives your readers action steps that they can take and use in their everyday lives. Think about ways to use this type of content to point out how you are different from your competitors.
4. **Don't be afraid to tell some of your secrets.** People love to hear about how to make something happen, and then they love to pay someone

else to do it. Let's be honest, even if someone just told us how to edit the code on our website to make it stick out like neon lights in a search engine, that doesn't mean we want to do it ourselves. Just give us a way to contact and hire you. After all, you just showed us you are the expert.

5. **Allow comments.** Consider allowing people to post comments about your blogs. In fact, you should be the first one to post a comment after each blog. Pose a question or comment to simply get a discussion started. If visitors are interacting and writing comments about your blog, they are actually adding relevant content that the search engines are going to like.

THEN, the real secret is to syndicate your blogs. Syndicating your blogs takes them and posts them on thousands of sites around the web, and they all link back to your original post, giving your website a "vote" in Google for relevance (which helps it to climb higher in the organic rankings), gives you another listing in the organic rankings for the subject that people are searching for (remember we talked about having multiple websites so you showed up multiple times for a certain subject in Google? Yes, this counts too!), and if you give them great content, it will also continue to build your expert status.

You can find some great blog syndication sources online just by typing "Blog Syndication" in Google.

3. Articles

Articles work the same way as blogs in regard to driving up the relevancy of your website in search engines. And while you should certainly use your articles in hard copy newsletters, etc, let's talk about them in the online world for a minute. The online game is content driven, so the more relevant content you have on a subject, the more likely you are to get traffic to your site. Articles allow you to show your expertise in a manner that is easily digestible to your visitors. The key to these articles, similar to blogs but slightly longer, is to keep them short and actionable. Give your potential clients information that they can use, and they will trust you even more -- getting you one step closer to earning their business.

Articles are usually a bit longer than blogs, but they don't have to be. Tell what you need to, but keep it slim. Remember, you are trying to build credibility as well, so try to keep your headline relevant to the context of your article. You should also keep your "sales pitches" (like "call me now to get started on your case!") to a minimum inside the content portion your article. *There's nothing worse than looking for good information on a topic, getting three sentences into an article and getting a blatant sales pitch.* Articles are meant to be informative, so try to leave the sales pitch out of the meat of the article and add a byline at the end. At the end of your articles, consider adding a section like this:

> **To learn more about Celebrity Branding® You, to lock out your competition, increase your profits, and have the practice you always dreamed of, visit www.CelebrityBrandingAgency. com. JW Dicks, Esq. and Nick Nanton, Esq. founders of the Celebrity Branding® Agency, publish the "Celebrity Branding You™" e-zine monthly covering topics that every lawyer looking to build their practice needs to know. If you're ready to take your practice to the next level, get more FREE info now at www. CelebrityBrandingAgency.com.**

This text can serve as your sales pitch. By adding in a link to your website, if you syndicate your article, you create additional inbound links to your site. Again, just run a Google search for "article syndication" and you'll find lots of sources.

4. Press Releases

This concept is easy, but most people miss it. So, you may want to read this part twice.

People do not know what you are doing unless you tell them.

It's as simple as that. Did you land a big settlement? Did your practice just celebrate its 20th anniversary? Are you under new management? Are you opening a new location? Are you involved in a charitable cause?

These are just a few of the questions that most of your clients would love to know. If they don't know, you simply aren't effectively communicating the answers. Having a "latest news" section on your website and in newsletters, where you can post press releases, allows you to post such items in a manner that makes them look like news, not like you're bragging about yourself. Write in the third person for these posts, and they will really keep your clients in the loop.

> *Note from Ben: Don't be shy about press releases. I used to think that waiting around for the media to call was the "right and proper" thing to do, Now, lawyers realize that they assist reporters in their jobs by providing them with a steady supply of relevant news or commentary on the law. Just do me one favor—forget about those "we are pleased to announce that John Doe has joined our office as an associate/partner" press releases. They are so boring that the only person who will want to read them is John's family!*

Not to mention, if you didn't already guess, you can syndicate the press releases for even more exposure! If you are using the same keywords, then you should start to dominate the first page of Google. Your competition will love it! (Just kidding!) And, of course it will make your potential clients' decision to contact you an obvious one.

5. Newsletters

Newsletters are "an oldie but a goodie." We're talking about real paper here people, the kind you have printed with ink that you can mail to your clients and prospects and hand out to everyone you meet.

A newsletter is really just a collection of information presented in any fashion you want. Some people choose to have them in color with bright photos on glossy paper, and others choose to print them on their laser printer in black and white with nothing but text. Both strategies work. The key factor to realize here is that it is a way to stay at the top of your clients' minds. With a newsletter, they will receive whatever information you want to give them at whatever time intervals you choose to give it to them.

WARNING: Be prepared for people to get absolutely hooked on your newsletter. We have heard several stories about clients calling to ask why they hadn't received their newsletters yet because they always look forward to them in their mailboxes at a certain time of the month! Wouldn't you like to build a huge list of these loyal fans?

There you have it, 5 of the many strategies that will have your clients and prospects learning everything you want them to know about you. Most importantly, you are building your reputation that you are the expert they should call when they need what you have to offer.

If you would like to learn more strategies we invite you to sign up for our free newsletters and magazines at **www.CelebrityBrandingAgency.com**. Building Celebrity status can grow your practice exponentially, so get started today!

About the Author:

Nick Nanton, Esq. is the co-founder of the Celebrity Branding® Agency. His company publishes the "Celebrity Branding You™" e-zine monthly, which covers topics that every lawyer looking to build their practice needs to know. For more information, visit www.CelebrityBrandingAgency.com.

Chapter 28

WIDGETS, TRINKETS, FREEBIES, HANDOUTS, TCHOTCHKES...

By: Michael Passov, Great Promo Items

Can something with names like these seriously and effectively advertise, promote and increase your practice...you bet they can! They are officially known as "advertising specialties", translation (mine not Webster's): a "special way to advertise." Consider that you are not just purchasing a mug, pen or t-shirt, you are buying "advertising space." A mug when imprinted with your information becomes a promotional item promoting *your* message.

There are numerous advantages to using imprinted promotional items. Here are just a few.

Cost

A law practice, with its short hours and hassle free clients, is lots of fun. I'm sure you all agree, but it's still a business. So, of course one of the first considerations is, what are these promotional items going to cost me? If used properly you'd be hard pressed to find a better return on your investment.

Take this simple example of ordering 1,000 magnetic memo boards custom printed in full color for around $1.00 each. You can include pictures, helpful information and highlight specific areas of your practice. It's a very useful item to stick on the refrigerator or file cabinet at home or office. They are easy to mail or can simply be handed out. You can quickly see how economically you can reach a lot of people. All it takes is one new client as a result of this effort, to more than pay for the entire order.

Longevity

Figuring very conservatively, if that memo board STICKS AROUND (pun intended) for two years and is only seen five times a day, your message will be viewed 3,650 times. Since all house guests migrate to the kitchen and most of us take more trips to the fridge than we care to admit, there's certain to be many more viewings than that. Please keep in mind that I am only following the life of one item for two years. After doing the math, the numbers become very favorable that your message will be seen over and over for a long period of time. There are thousands of items that can be interchanged with this example. How many times have you heard someone (or maybe yourself) embarrassed or bragging about how many years they (you) have had the same t-shirt?

Visabilty

Once again if you retain the concept that you are buying advertising space, then dollar for dollar promotional items give you the best bang for your buck. Other forms of advertising, such as newspaper, TV or radio, are many times not read, seen or heard by those reading, watching or listening. Even if the message does get noticed they are most times soon forgotten. It is even more evident if your service is not something they need at the time. Of course, if you have the money to fund a strong ongoing media campaign they can be very successful. The problem is most businesses don't have the type of money needed to properly implement one. When is the last time you walked down the street, looked around your office or house "without" seeing a hat, shirt, mug or a number of other items with a company name. This type of visibility for your firm is hard to find.

Tarket Marketing

Another great advantage is that you can easily target who you want to receive your message. Whether it's intended for clients, prospective clients or a group in which you seek referrals, you have the control. If you want to target seniors you can give them a magnifying bookmark. This bookmark will help them to read things that many struggle with in their daily lives and clearly see your imprinted message. You can even add the line *"When it comes to your Legal Matters we can Help you with the Fine Print."* So you can target a specific market while giving them something they will use and appreciate.

Target Location

You can even target the location the item will be used. Let's say you want to be known as "The Law Firm" to call in case of an auto accident. It would obviously be advantageous to them (and you) to have your name and phone number handy when an accident occurs.

You can give out a number of things the recipients would keep on their person or in the car. A key chain, or something to put on the key chain, is definitely a location you would like your name and number to be found. Make sure they would have a reason to use what you give them. One example of this would be a key chain with a bright LED light. We work with many law firms and have actually developed a very cost effective way to get their name and numbers on thousands of key chains. It's called the Lost Keys Program and helps those who lose their keys dramatically increase their chances of having them returned. The "key" point here is that you are giving them a reason to use the item in a location that is good for both of you. Emergency kits, ice scrapers, visor clips to hold sunglasses are items to secure a location in the car.

Set The Tone

Whether your marketing takes on a serious or a humorous tone, promotional products can enhance those efforts. If you do wills, trusts and estate planning you can give out foam rubber stress relievers. Include a message like *"Preparing to Protect Your Family doesn't have to be a Stressful Ordeal."* Another option is to give a document organizer with the message *"We Can Help You Organize Your Estate to Protect Your Family."*

Improves Results

To be successful you have to have a goal and a plan to get there. Using promotional items is no different. Many think that simply getting imprinted pens will be a great way to advertise. When delivered, they think how cool it is to have their name on a pen. They excitedly hand them out to their office associates, family and friends *who would have used their services anyway*. Then it hits them "what do I do with the rest?" Unfortunately the remainder may end up in storage.

Now take those same pens, but this time with a goal to **bring in more accident cases**. The plan is to spread the word with a mailing that will grab attention. Studies show that the use of a promotional item in a mailing creates greater impact and produces better results than one without. Mail the pens with a letter talking about your experience and success in representing accident cases. Be sure to highlight cases you have obtained sizable settlements for.

Note from Ben: As with any other type of marketing, a real key is to do something "different" from your competition. For example, my mastermind member Vaughan DeKirby came up with the "key tag" program as a way of convincing the recipient of the key tag to actually place it on their key ring. This program ensures that if your client's keys are lost then found, that YOU will be the one to help get the keys back to the owner. Brilliant!

Our own promotional pens aren't the usual "Law Offices of Ben Glass, here's our phone number." Instead, the imprint is:

Confused by Lawyer Ads?
TheTruthAboutLawyerAds.com
Injured and Getting Calls?
TheAccidentbook.com
Talk to Ben Glass 703-591-9829

Chapter 29

DIFFERENTIATION — HOW A FORMER INSURANCE DEFENSE ATTORNEY SEPARATES HIMSELF FROM THE PACK

By: James Parrish, The Parrish Law Firm (TheParrishLawFirm.com)

In this era of mass competition and everybody trying to look like everybody else (for example, have you ever noticed how all of the new shopping centers, restaurants, gas stations, etc., in Texas look just like the ones you find in Virginia?), you must be DIFFERENT from your competition in order to succeed. Otherwise, you give your potential client pool no compelling reason to use your services or buy your products.

So, as you are creating, or re-creating, your business, you need to come up with ways to differentiate yourself from the other folks in your field. CREATE AN OVERWHELMING DESIRE WITHIN PEOPLE FOR WHAT YOU OFFER! For example, in my personal injury law practice, I have chosen to highlight the fact that I formerly worked for the insurance companies for a number of years and know those companies from the inside out. In fact, I have deemed myself to be the "insurance insider" and focus the vast majority of my marketing activities around this persona.

The message that I am sending to potential clients is that I am unique in that I now represent people who are injured and facing insurance companies, but in the past worked for those same insurance companies. My potential clients understand that I know the way that insurance companies function and understand that I will not allow them to be subject to the normal insurance tricks of the trade, which take advantage of many, many injured folks during the personal injury claims process. Therefore, my message to the market of potential clients is not your standard personal injury lawyer shtick, which can usually be found in a Yellow Pages ad with words like "I care about you and there will not be a fee unless there is a recovery." Again, my point of differentiation is that "I used to work for the insurance companies and please allow me to use my inside information to your benefit against those companies in your claim." See the difference?

As you begin working on your differentiating business description and message, you need to develop the information that will help you answer the question, which you will inevitably receive from a potential client, "What makes you different from the rest of the lawyers (doctors, contractors, etc.) out there?" or "Why should I use you instead of Joe the lawyer down the street?"

This differentiation process is extremely important and is something that you must work on, develop, massage, and ultimately refine if you want to market and sell your business to its fullest extent. So sit down with a pen and a pad and begin writing the skills that you have which you believe separate you from the rest of your market. Then look around on the Internet for competitors in your field (and others) and compare what it is that they are offering to that unique skill set that you have written down. From there, you will be able to see the qualities and skills which make you different and you will be well on your well to developing your "differentiating" message.

About the Author:

James Parrish is a Northern Virginia injury lawyer and founder of the Parrish Law Firm. He is a graduate of the University of Virginia. Mr. Parrish is a former partner in one of the oldest trial law firms in Northern Virginia. He is also a former member of Ben Glass's elite lawyer marketing master mind group.

Chapter 30

BUT, BEN, MY DUI PRACTICE IS DIFFERENT!

By: Bob Battle, Richmond, Virginia DUI Lawyer (BobBattleLaw.com)

Note from Ben Glass: In my opinion, Richmond, Virginia DUI lawyer Bob Battle is the premier expert on how to successfully market a DUI/traffic practice. Battle has cracked the code on how to market and automate his practice and his results show that he has 'refused to participate in the recession!' It hasn't always been that way for Bob's business. Prior to attending his first Great Legal Marketing ("GLM") seminar in the Spring of 2006, his practice struggled mightily. I have asked Bob to share his story and insights which reveal that the direct response marketing techniques work at least as well if not better in an area of law that is extremely time sensitive.

*After attending the seminar, Bob niched his practice to focus on **DUI** and **Reckless Driving Speeding** defense. Bob's big breakthrough was to abandon typical lawyer advertising. For example, he totally avoids Yellow Pages ads and he does not advertise on either the national lawyer or DUI directories online. You won't find him on billboards, on television or on the radio. Nevertheless, over the last 18 months, he's managed to triple his income of high quality DUI cases, increase his yearly gross income from $170,000.00 to over $440,000.00, raise his fees by 70 percent to $5,000.00 per first offense DUI, get featured on CNN, the CBS Evening News, the Baltimore Sun* *and the Washington Times, all while reducing his workweek from over 60 hours a week to right now around 31."*

The Road To Truly Effective Marketing

The biggest breakthrough in marketing my DUI and Reckless Driving Speeding practice was learning how to do effective marketing. I am not talking about lawyer marketing; I am talking about truly effective marketing, and there is a big difference. A lot of the concepts I am going to be talking about are probably completely new and foreign to you, but they work tremendously. They have not only completely transformed my DUI practice, but they have transformed my life. In addition to the exponential increase in income, I can honestly say that the last 18 months have been by far and away the most fun I have had in my 23 years of practicing law.

Background

I grew up in Alexandria, Virginia, went to college at the University of Notre Dame and went to law school at William and Mary. After finishing law school in the Spring of 1984, I was lucky enough to get a clerkship with United States District Court Judge James Cacheris in Alexandria, Virginia- the famous "Rocket Docket" of the Eastern District of Virginia. I later was a prosecutor in Fairfax County, Virginia, for the most famous prosecutor in the history of Virginia, Bob Horan, in one of the busiest offices in the country. Since leaving the office in 1990, I have either been a solo or with one other partner. A huge change occurred in my practice and my life in 1999 when I got married and moved from Alexandria to Richmond, Virginia. Richmond is 100 miles south of where I had grown up and where I had established a practice. At this point in my career, I realized I really needed to learn how to market to get clients coming in the door consistently.

One of my biggest pet peeves with law school education is that law school does not spend one second teaching students how to run a business or market their practice. The reality is that most law school professors have never had to run a successful business or successfully market their business. Law school spends plenty of time telling you what you can't do in marketing, but no time teaching marketing principles that work.

Furthermore, it doesn't matter what your credentials are- there are countless examples of lawyers that believe that their diploma, skill, and competence are all it takes to build a thriving practice. In reality, it does not matter what law school you graduated from, how many hours you have logged, or how many cases you have won. Without a sound, reliable, predictable system for attracting a constant stream of new clients, you will starve.

Misadventures in "RC" and "MSMD" Marketing

Although I am able to laugh at myself now, when I first arrived in Richmond, I was making the same mistakes that I see just about every other lawyer make in using the Yellow Pages reps and the lawyer directory reps as my primary marketing sources. (Ben Glass refers to these reps collectively as "the marketing vultures.") I like to say that initially, I was practicing RC marketing. "RC" stands for random chance. That means you sit in your office staring at the phone and praying that it is going to ring or hoping that any minute someone will walk in the door by random chance and say they desperately need your help. Believe me, more people don't walk in than do walk in. Those that did walk in were looking for the lowest price, too.

Next, I decided I needed to do some more advertising to get the word out so I switched my strategy from RC marketing to a much more ingenious strategy which I call MSMD marketing. "MSMD" stands for "Monkey See, Monkey Do." I looked at what other lawyers were doing and just copied them. I paid for a Yellow Pages ad and put my bio up on the various lawyer websites and directory websites, gave a ton of money to these reps and I figured that since that is what everybody else was doing, it must work, right? Wrong. As a general proposition, if you are doing the same exact type of marketing as everyone else, by definition your marketing is average at best.

One of the biggest problems with the lawyer directory sites is that, for the vast majority of them, the only criteria to get listed is to have a credit card and a pulse. Also, most of them are just delivering overpriced Google ad words and/or Superpages.com results. But even more importantly, and the reason I don't have my name associated with any of these sites is that they are very often misleading. One DUI directory in its advertising to recruit lawyers, states that anyone can be a DUI lawyer since DUI defendants are scared, have lots of money and most of the cases plead guilty anyway. Another lawyer directory talks about getting local attorneys where there is only one attorney for the entire state.

I honestly think that Yellow Pages advertising is a dying franchise. A potential attorney advertiser just has to look at the economic realities and has to ask themselves one important question: Who is my ideal client? The ideal client for a DUI Lawyer is someone with a pending DUI charge who doesn't have another lawyer already and who can afford your fees. The people who are still "letting their fingers do the walking" through the Yellow Pages do not have, as a group, the same amount of money that the people who are looking through the Internet or in other areas do. Of course, the Yellow Pages rep will tell you that the solution is buy a bigger ad and throw more money at the problem. Yeah, right! Today, I do not spend a dime on the Yellow Pages.

Let me make it clear that I was making money and was never in danger of not being able to pay my bills, but there were months where I did not pay myself or everything went directly to Uncle Sam. As a true solo practitioner, I was grossing in excess of $150,000 per year, but I just did not have a steady, reliable stream of clients and income coming in, which I like to call "sleep at night business." What I am referring to is the feeling that, when you go to bed every night, you do not have to worry that the phone will ring or that you will have an abundance of paying clients. I knew at the time that to make the money that I was making that I needed to constantly grind it out and grind it out and work on weekends and, if I ever "eased up on the gas" even the slightest bit, that this stream of money coming in would dry up instantly. Needless to say, my stress level was tremendous. At the time, my wife, Ellen, a local family doctor, wanted to cut back on her work schedule after the birth of our second child, but stated that she could not since my income was so unpredictable and fluctuated so much. Ouch!

Great Legal Marketing to the Rescue

In the spring of 2006, I signed up for Ben Glass' Great Legal Marketing seminar in Fairfax, Virginia. Ben is a Fairfax, Virginia personal injury and medical malpractice lawyer and an incredible authority on effective, ethical and importantly outside the box legal marketing. So I signed up for this seminar. Let me tell you, it was expensive and at the time I did not have a lot of extra money and it was not a bar sponsored seminar for CLE credit, but I can tell you that there is absolutely no doubt that making the decision to invest in this seminar was the greatest business decision I have or will ever make in my career.

Here are some of the huge take-aways from my first seminar:

Riches in Niches

This marketing truism applies to all businesses. By niching one's business, it is easier to present a laser sharp marketing message to potential clients and to demonstrate your expertise. As a former prosecutor who also had experience with civil personal injury cases, I was holding myself out as handling any criminal, traffic or personal injury case in state or federal court. At the GLM conference, I learned the Pareto Principle, also referred to as the 80-20 Principle. This rule states that, for many events, roughly 80% of the effects come from 20% of the causes. Applied to my law business, this principle states that 80% of your income comes from 20% of your clients. Similarly that 80% of your aggravation comes from 20% of your clients, etc. The key is to critically evaluate your business and focus on those 20% of your clients who bring the greatest return and get rid of the 20% that cause you the most aggravation. For me, it was easy- I really liked my DUI and traffic clients. They were good people who made a mistake. I also was able to get a large number of my DUI clients to honestly evaluate whether they had an alcohol problem and to get them help while also delivering great results in court. My Reckless Driving Speeding practice saves hundreds of people a year from winding up with a permanent criminal record and dealing with all the unfair insurance and employment consequences.

On the other hand, my federal court-appointed criminal clients were a pain in the butt, for little money, no gratitude and a ton of aggravation. There is a perception among criminal defendants that if you are taking court-appointed cases, you are an inexperienced, incompetent lawyer. It took a ton of work to stay on top of the latest federal criminal rulings on the Sentencing Guidelines alone and most defendants were incarcerated over an hour from Richmond and could not be contacted by phone. Likewise, even potential retained clients who wanted to see me for serious felony crimes rarely turned out to have any money, and ultimately went with the Public Defender. Most of these people were finding me from my Yellow Pages ad and the conversation always went like this, " My boyfriend is locked up and charged with (drug dealing, burglary, grand larceny, etc.). What would you charge to represent him?" This question was usually the only one asked! What a waste of time.

After doing my 80/20 evaluation, I removed myself from all court appointed lists, stopped spending time marketing for other types of criminal cases or personal injury cases and focused on DUI and Reckless Driving Speeding cases. By niching, I am able to easily stay on top of all DUI and traffic issues in Virginia and nationwide. I have even been told by other lawyers that my Virginia DUI Lawyer Blog (www.VirginiaDUILawyerBlog.com) and Blog on my website (www.BobBattleLaw.com) are a "valuable public service." Also, as I mentioned, I bid hasta la vista to the Yellow Pages for good. By niching, I am a better lawyer, a happier, less stressed lawyer and I have a practice that is much easier to market to potential clients.

Focus on the Internet; Focus on the Client

The Internet is where 80% of new cases are going to be coming from and really the key is to find and create a website that consistently shows up on Page 1 of Google for relevant searches. First, I needed to be on Page 1 of Google so I searched and searched and searched until I finally found the best website developer out there who developed a website for me that regularly and consistently shows up on Page 1 of Google for all the relevant search terms for Richmond area "DUI" or "Reckless Driving Speeding" lawyer. Ben Glass'

Webmaster, Tom Foster, was also a presenter at the GLM conference. I checked out the results his clients were getting, including Ben Glass, and knew he could deliver the promised land- Page 1 of Google. I signed on with Foster Web Marketing and that, as Bogie's character Rick said to Louis in Casablanca, was the beginning of a beautiful friendship! Read more about Tom Foster and Foster Web Marketing in Chapter 16-Stop Whining: Making Your Website Really Work for You.

The second breakthrough change that I learned was that the entire focus of my marketing was in the wrong direction; it was all ego driven as opposed to client driven and being focused on what the client is thinking about. So in that respect, I set about to completely redo the way my website spoke to clients and also to create education based marketing by writing consumer guides and books. In order to accomplish this task, Ben Glass stressed that you must "enter into the conversation" the potential client was already having in their head. I already knew what was on the potential client's mind since I had already been practicing law for over 2 decades at this point and had spoken with thousands of clients at that point in my career.

Education Based Marketing: Books and Consumer Guides

As I mentioned, in addition to having far more content on my website than other DUI/Traffic lawyers, I have created education-based books and made them available on my website for my two major practice areas, DUI and Reckless Driving Speeding defense. The DUI book is titled *How to Choose a DUI Lawyer in Virginia*. Being the author of this book not only makes me the instant celebrity, but it also gives me great credibility. I am delivering important information that the potential client will find nowhere else. I talk about the problems with other lawyer directories or some of the other B.S. I see on the Internet or mistakes that I see lawyers make that cost their client from being able to win a case. By providing this type of valuable inside knowledge, I have developed this great credibility and trust with the clients right off the bat. Building credibility is crucial, especially since we all know what the public's general perception of lawyers is on the trust scale. (On surveys of what the public's general perception is of different professions for being "trustworthy," lawyers are usually embarrassingly low- usually slightly below "Used Car Salesman" and just edging out "Somali Pirate!")

My other consumer guide on my website is titled "The Shocking Truth about Reckless Driving Speeding in Virginia." The primary purpose of this guide is to educate the public about the fact that Virginia makes Reckless Driving Speeding a serious criminal offense with potentially devastating collateral consequences for their insurance, their license, and their careers.

In addition to making yourself the instant expert, providing this information through a book/consumer guide is an incredibly powerful way to tell a client about your practice and to persuade subtly, as opposed to giving some sort of a slick sales pitch to get the client to hire the lawyer. Thus, there is no pressure whatsoever on the client- no lawyer sticking a retainer agreement in their face and trying to get them to sign on the dotted line. In fact the entire message on my website is that the potential client should read these books **before** talking to anyone, including me.

What makes this concept of book authorship work is that I provide a lot of really valuable content and information, but at the same time I am also establishing the "buying criteria." When I talk about buying criteria in the context of a lawyer or law practice, I am talking about how the potential client winds up hiring a lawyer. This concept is important because the people who are looking for a lawyer on the Internet really do not have any idea how to choose a DUI lawyer. They do not know who is good or who is one of these "dump truck" DUI lawyers who signed on to become a DUI lawyer to plead people guilty. Most importantly, prior to reading my books, they do not know how to differentiate the two. They have never had to hire a DUI lawyer before so they flounder around and often make a bad decision. So by educating them, you can not only guide them but also guide them towards you. This low-pressure means of providing valuable free information lets the client reach their own conclusion that you are the best lawyer for their case.

Develop Systems and Automate

The key to my website is that both of these consumer guides are delivered free and instantly. Thus, the book becomes a key point of my overall system, and I have made it a central focus of my website to convince the potential client to "raise their hand" and get the book. I have tested multiple layouts of web pages to see which ones get more potential customers to request the consumer guides. After the potential client has read the book, they have often already made the decision that they want to hire me. The key feature of my system is that it works on autopilot. So, when someone comes to my website, they hear from me via my video on the site. When they request one of my books, it is automatically sent to them. There is an automatic follow-up email delivered simultaneously with the book. There is also another email letter that occurs automatically a couple days later. All of this activity occurs without me even having entered the equation yet. So my system is fully implemented and every week, I spend my time talking to people who have already made up their mind that they are going to hire me or are strongly leaning towards hiring me if they can afford my services before they have even spoken with me. So, contrast my current position with every other lawyer's situation. I regularly get people calling me, hoping I will take their case instead of the typical situation of the lawyer hoping the client will hire them.

And They Lived Happily Ever After

As you can probably guess, if you fast-forward to 2010, my wife does work only 3 days a week and acknowledges that, economically, she does not need to work at all. She works because she loves being a family doctor. My hours have been cut drastically, while gross revenue is up almost 3 times what it was just 3 years ago. I now coach DUI lawyers on marketing in Virginia and I am expanding the coaching nationwide. We have built a second dream house in Wintergreen, Virginia while most others are still reeling from the recession. When my wife first met Ben Glass, she told him "You have changed our lives." And, yes, I do have a "sleep at night business," thank you! Congratulations on reading this book- it is your first step to getting rid of your nightmare practice and making all your wildest dreams come true.

About the Author:

Bob Battle is a Richmond Virginia DUI and Reckless Driving/Speeding Lawyer. His practice is solely devoted to serious traffic defense and criminal litigation in state and federal courts. He has been quoted in The Washington Post and The Washington Times as a legal expert. Mr. Battle frequently lectures other lawyers at educational seminars by such groups as the Virginia Trial Lawyers Association and Virginia CLE. Visit his website at BobBattleLaw.com

Chapter 31

PAY PER CLICK ADVERTISING FOR LAWYERS
What is Pay-Per-Click Advertising?
By Timothy Seward, ROI Revolution

Advertising With Control: Pay-Per-Click advertising (or PPC) is a unique form of online advertising that gives advertisers of all sizes a chance to bid on keywords typed into major search engines and have their ad appear. The most distinctive feature of this advertising model is that businesses only have to pay when their ad is actually clicked on.

Getting Started: Each search engine has a different Pay-Per-Click program; however, it makes sense to start your ads off in the search engine that has the highest search volume; Google. Then, as you see that PPC is working for your practice, you can expand to Yahoo, MSN (Bing), and other engines.

Most engines charge a very small fee (usually less than $5.00) to activate your account, and then of course you only pay for clicks that your ads generate. Here are the links to the major search engine's advertising programs:

Google: AdWords.Google.com
Yahoo: SearchMarketing.Yahoo.com
Bing/MSN: Advertising.Microsoft.com

Why Pay-Per-Click Advertising Makes Sense for Lawyers:

Pay-Per-Click For Lawyers? There are many reasons why Pay-Per-Click advertising is a great fit for lawyers. There is no other advertising form available that lets you control so many aspects of your campaigns such as how much you spend, what audience you target, when your campaigns are active, and where your ads show. No matter what marketing channels you are currently using, PPC advertising can supplement those, and provide an entirely new source of client leads to your firm.

Qualified "Hand Picked" Leads. With PPC, you pick the keywords for which your ads show for, the location (or geo-targeting) that your ads are shown, the amount you spend, and the messaging that is shown. This allows you to filter out cases you don't want before they actually get to your firm, essentially creating a "hand picked" lead generation system that is designed around your individual needs.

Pay-Per-Click 101. There are several factors that are key to running successful PPC campaigns. In the next few pages of this chapter, you'll learn the most important tips and tricks for setting up Pay-Per-Click campaigns to market your law firm. We'll get down to the basics and core concepts that are essential in bringing you the right leads. Setting up your online campaigns properly from the start will save you $100's in advertising spend.

On the next few pages we will discuss:

- Geographic Targeting
- Campaign Structure
- How to Choose the Right Keywords
- Free Keyword Resources
- Writing Powerful Ad Text
- What is a Destination URL, and how do you choose it?
- Tracking Performance
- AdWords Reports 101

More Information: After reading this chapter, if you are interested in learning more about Pay-Per-Click advertising, there are many resources online that can supplement what we will discuss. Google AdWords offers a great learning center which starts at the very basics and covers all subjects in video tutorials. The learning center is entirely free and you can access it by visiting: Google.com/adwords/learningcenter.

Geo Targeting: Zoning in on the Leads & Cases You Want

One of the most important settings in your Pay-Per-Click account is geo-targeting. This will control where in the United States (or the world) your ads will show. Most Pay-Per-Click advertising models give you several targeting options. You can focus on entire cities, or you can enter in your zip code and show ads within a certain number of miles around your physical address.

To determine how to set your geo-targeting, just think about how far away from your office you want to take cases. Do you only want to work on cases from the city where you are located, or would you be willing to work with clients in neighboring cities as well? Whatever location you decide to target you should extend this about 15-30 miles out. Many people will be searching for an Attorney at work, while they live in another area.

To customize the geo-targeting options in your Google AdWords account, simply go to the "Settings" tab of the campaign you wish to edit and click "Edit" underneath the locations section:

A map will then appear where you can enter the physical address of your practice, and also the distance around your practice that you want your ads to show.

> *Bonus Tip* You should check the box that says "Allow address to show in ads", as this will add a line underneath your ads with your firm's physical address, making your ad stand out from your competitor's.

Campaign Structure

As mentioned earlier, most PPC advertising platforms are very similar. There are certain settings that vary per search engine; however, if you understand the basic structure that I'm about to go over, then you'll be in good shape when it comes to setting up your campaigns, regardless of the network.

Account: The account level is where you enter your personal information, including your company information, phone number, and billing information.

Campaign: The campaign is the top level of your account. This is where geo targeting, budgets, and many advanced settings will be set.

Ad Group: Each ad group contains a set of keywords, and ad text that is associated with those keywords.

Choosing The Right Keywords

The Basics: Keywords are the root of all of your Pay-Per-Click traffic. A keyword is the word or phrase that a user types into Google when they are searching for something. The keywords in your campaigns can contain one word, or in some extreme cases up to four or five phrases (called long-tail keywords). It's best to have a mix of both of these types of keywords in your account.

Building Your Initial Keyword List: To start developing your keywords, think about what potential clients would ideally type into Google when looking for your services. Some of the more general, most obvious keywords will be the most expensive, but if you take the time to build out long tail keywords, these keywords will most always be less competitive and less expensive.

Here is an example of taking a very broad Keyword:

"Personal Injury Lawyer"

If you add in some location qualifiers, suddenly the competition gets a little slimmer:

"Personal Injury Lawyer in Atlanta, GA"
Don't forget to bid on your zip code:
"Personal Injury Lawyer 28029"

Grouping Your Keywords: You will need to group like keywords together in the same ad group. This is because ad text is associated at the ad group level; therefore, all keywords in the same ad group will share the same ads. If your firm specializes in three different kinds of law, it's a good idea to start off with an ad group for each type of law:

You can see above how all the keywords in the "personal injury" ad group have "personal injury" in the keyword, and that theory applies to both ad groups above. Having tightly themed ad groups takes time to initially build out, but will benefit you greatly as you write relevant ad text. Having tightly themed ad groups can also help you manage your bids and more effectively.

Negative Keywords: Negative keywords are words or phrases for which you do not want your ad to show for. Having the proper negative keywords in place can save you $100's in advertising spend. Here are a few negatives that most lawyers will want in their accounts:

- Scholarship
- Salary

- Joke/Jokes
- University
- Job description
- Quote/quotes
- Dictionary
- Pictures
- Bad
- Education

You most likely would not want your ads to show for the query **"lawyer jokes"** or **"lawyer salary"**, so it's very important to add negative keywords to your account.

When you specify negative keywords, Google will no longer show your ads for any keyword variations that contain the negative keywords that you have listed in your account. Adding negative keywords can improve your lead quality dramatically.

Branded Terms: It's important to have a "branded" campaign that contains variations of your name, the name of your law firm, your attorneys' names, and your website URL.

This will help guarantee that your competitors do not outbid you on your own terms, it will also separate these highly profitable keywords from your other terms, which will prevent your overall account statistics from being skewed.

You may be wondering, "Why should I pay for a listing if my site is already displaying organically?" If you appear twice, searchers are more likely to find your practice. Also, this stops competitors from snagging your traffic if they are bidding on your branded terms and you aren't.

Also, if you don't have high organic ranking, then you can use you paid campaigns to have your practice appear on the first page of the search results.

You will want to bid on all versions of your firm's name including:

- Common misspellings
- Your firm's domain
- Your firm's URL
- Your attorney's names

For example, let's say your practice is called Wilsons Law Firm; you would want to bid on the following keywords as well as other variations:

- Wilsons Law Firm
- Wilson Law Firm
- Wilson's Law Firm
- Wilsonslawfirm
- www.wilsonlawfirm.com
- Wilsonlawfirm

Free Keyword Resources

There are tons of free resources on the web that can help you create your keyword lists. Our favorites are as follows:

AdWords Keyword Tool: This is a free tool that Google offers which helps you discover new keywords and build your keyword list. You enter keywords you are interested in and it spits back synonyms and average search volumes:

Keyword Combiner: This tool takes keyword lists and combines them for you. This is a huge time saver, and easier than doing the task in excel. Just Google "keyword combiner" to find this tool.

SpyFu.com: Simply enter in your competitors' domain and see a list of terms they are bidding on! Of course this is not 100% accurate, but it's pretty close. It's a great way to get new keyword ideas.

Get ROI's Ultimate Guide to Writing Ads: Get ad writing tips and best-practices that we've developed from years of experience distilled into one powerful cheat-sheet. To receive our brand new **"PPC Ad Writing Quick-Reference Guide",** visit www.roirevolution.com/writingads.

Writing Powerful Ad Text

Enter Conversation in Searcher's Mind: Since a searcher on Google already knows what they are looking for, it's important to write your ads in a way that enters the conversation that is taking place in the searcher's mind. Think about what the searcher wants and what questions they are asking, and use your ad text to address those needs.

Differentiate Your Practice: Since competition is fierce on many legal terms, it's important to study your competitors' ads and make sure your ad creatives stand out from theirs. What sets you apart? Are you the most experienced lawyer? Most convenient? Do you win most of your cases? Are you the most affordable? Whatever makes you different, make sure your ad text emphasizes this.

Call To Action: Now that you've gotten the searcher's attention by differentiating yourself from every other ad on the page, you need to add a call to action to your ad text. Here are a few examples of call to actions that Lawyers typically use:

- Sign Up For Our Free Report
- Free Consultation
- Free Divorce Price Calculator
- Free Case Review

The Power of Two: Since ads are set at the ad group level, it is best practice to always have two ads active in each ad group. The reason you will want to do this is so you can always test two ads against each other. Test different headlines, body copy, calls to actions and more.

You'll want to compare the **conversion rates** and **click-through rate**s to figure out which ad is performing better. Also be sure to let enough data gather before you begin to draw conclusions about the tests. By constantly testing ads, you are continually improving the performance of your campaigns.

What is a Destination URL, and how do you choose it?

There are two types of URL's in Google AdWords:

1. **Display URL:** This is the URL that appears at the bottom of your ad, which can be modified as long as it contains your main root URL. This means you can add words to the beginning or end of the URL to make it more relevant to the keyword being searched. For examples, If your URL is RobersonLaw.com. you can modify your display URL to read RobersonLaw.com/**Injury** to make it more relevant to the personal injury keywords.
2. **Destination URL:** This is the actual page on your firm's website site that your ad is pointing to. You will want this to be as relevant to the keyword and ad as possible. This page is often times referred to as a landing page.

What should you use as your Destination URL? It's almost never a good idea to use your home page as your destination URL. Having a special landing page developed for each area of law you practice is a good start. All of the information on these pages should be specific to the area of law that the landing page is promoting

The last thing you want is for visitors to have to hunt around your website looking for the information they need to decide to choose you as their lawyer. Make it easy for potential clients to find what they need. Cut out unnecessary text and focus on the information that is most important.

Make an Irresistible Offer: One of the most powerful ways to draw new leads is to write a free "mini-book" on your expertise. Offer your clients free information on the type of law you practice. In exchange for the free report or mini book, you will collect the client's mailing address and email address.

Landing Page Checklist: Here are a few things that will help potential clients decide to choose you as their lawyer:

- ✓ Testimonials
- ✓ Free reports/Widgets
- ✓ Several Ways to Contact You (phone number, e-mail, quick contact form)
- ✓ A video of yourself
- ✓ Free Consultation form
- ✓ Success Stories
- ✓ Online Chat options
- ✓ Information on the Area of Law you practice
- ✓ Certifications
- ✓ Legal Glossary (specific to that area of law)

    Bonus Tip If you've already got landing pages setup and you are looking to improve them, Google offers a free tool that lets you test different aspects of your page. You can easily test elements such as color, headlines, call to actions, buttons and much more. To lean more about this free tool visit: Google.com/websiteoptimizer.

Tracking Your Campaigns

What is a conversion? A conversion is any action on your website that you want the visitor to take. This can be filling out a lead, downloading a free report, or clicking on a certain page of your site. Tracking these conversions is very important to understand how your campaigns are performing.

Before you take any campaigns live, it's crucial to get a tracking system in place that will allow you to monitor which campaigns and keywords are bringing in leads and which are spending money without converting into leads for you.

Tracking Option 1 (Basic): Conversion Tracking

Each engine offers free conversion tracking with their PPC accounts that is fairly easy to setup. Basically, you'll take a snippet of code and paste it on your receipt page for your websites conversion. If you have several conversions on your landing pages, then you will paste the tracking script on all thank you pages (or receipt pages) that are on your site.

Tracking Option 2 (Advanced): Google Analytics

Google Analytics is a powerful free web analytics service that Google offers. We won't go into detail on how to set it up in this chapter; however, it offers advanced reports on your websites visitors, traffic, pages, and more. To learn more visit: google.com/analytics

Use Both! Many people actually use both AdWords conversion tracker and Analytics together for even more advanced reporting.

Google AdWords Reports 101

AdWords offers a ton of free reports that allow you to monitor the performance of your campaigns. You can even schedule these reports to run automatically and be sent to your e-mail address. There are few "top reports" that are crucial for managing your account's performance.

You can view most of these metrics in the AdWords interface; however, sometimes it's easier to access this information in a report and manipulate the data in excel. It's really a personal preference which option you select.

Placement/Keyword Report: This report outlines your keyword performance over a specific period of time. You can see metrics such as cost, conversions, and cost-per-conversion. Sorting by spend allows you to see keywords that were costing you a ton and did not convert at all for you. Of course, you will want to bid these keywords down. You can also sort by conversions to see keywords that are converting, but are not in the top positions. You'll want to bid these keywords up.

Ad Performance Report: Use this report to analyze the performance of your ad text. By pausing ads that are not performing well, you can dramatically increase the click through rate and conversion rate of your account. You'll want to focus on click-through-rate and conversion rate when analyzing this campaign.

URL Performance Report: This report analyzes the performance of your landing pages. Use this to see overall statistics on which landing page is performing the best.

Get 50 More Expert AdWords Tactics

We hope that this chapter has inspired you to learn more about Google AdWords and how you can use it to market your practice. If you are interested in learning more about how to drive more response and profit from your AdWords account, we'd like to offer you 50 more expert tips in our 16 page pocket guide.

In this guide, you'll get our best 50 AdWords secrets, tactics and strategies designed to make you such a profitable advertiser, that eventually you'll consider hiring us to run your AdWords campaign to scale your profits even higher.

To receive our new 16-page pocket guide **"50 Ways To Make Your AdWords Advertising Drive More Response and More Profit"** simply visit www.roirevolution.com/google-adwords /ppc-free-resources.php and fill out the form after the video.

Whether you are starting from scratch, or you currently have an AdWords account that needs some tweaks we hope you are encouraged to learn more about Pay-Per-Click advertising and how you can use it to create a customized lead generation tool to market your firm.

FREQUENTLY ASKED QUESTIONS

What's with the "BengieBoy SuperMan Cape Thing?"

Lots of people want to know about the origin of the cartoon that has me in a "Super Hero" cape. Does it mean I can leap tall buildings and repel bullets for my clients?

No, nothing as silly as that.

The cartoon comes from a photograph that I came across in one of those family albums we have from when I was little. There I was, with my brother Tom in front of the fireplace at my house in Annandale, Virginia, with my brand new "SuperMan"™ costume. That gave me an idea for a newsletter article but it wasn't on idea about "being super." The cartoon is all about when we were little kids and we _knew_ that anything was possible. We played "super hero" games (and cops and robbers and cowboys and Indians) and no one told us that we couldn't be whatever we wanted. As we grew older, however, those "voices out there" start to implant in our heads the idea that "but you have to remember reality" and "no, you can't have everything."

Well, that's total bull and the BengieBoy cartoon is a constant reminder that "yes, darn it, you can do anything." Don't let the mediocre majority convince you otherwise.

Ben and his brother Tom, Ready to Save the World

If your law practice is so successful why do you teach marketing? Everywhere I turn I see a new "lawyer marketing guru" running seminars, offering product and sending e-mails.

First, as my friend Dan Kennedy pointed out in a recent issue of his No B. S. Newsletter, "you are right to question the proliferation of gurus, but you ought to be very happy there are so many legitimate ones who followed a path I laid out, to package up their successful methodology in diverse, specific fields and make it available within those industries to peers."

Second, you ask a fair question. The last few years have certainly seen an explosion of legal marketing and practice consultants, seminar and teleseminar givers and a variety of self-appointed gurus, some "certified," selling themselves and their information to other lawyers because they must. Their incomes from their core businesses never existed, have recently vanished or are slipping away, so hey, why not be a marketing guru? They see others doing it, maybe even attend one or two of their seminars or marketing conferences to see what's going on, set up a website and whammo, they are in business. Most have never actually risked a dime marketing and running their own law practice. Others practiced law at some point in the (sometimes very distant) past. I have no intention of selling my practice or retiring from the practice of law. Truth is, I like being a lawyer and I'm proud of the work that I do for my clients.

I definitely do not need your money this week to pay last week's bills or at all and I've not created some big fat mess of overhead with staff and seminars and teleseminars all over the place to support infrastructure, nor do I have the time or desire to send three emails a week, all pitching the next great thing (i.e.

something else that I can sell you.) You probably know my story by now. I am a practicing personal injury and medical malpractice attorney in Fairfax, Virginia. I started my own solo practice in 1995 after working for and with someone else for 12 years. I've got a small office about six miles from my house and just a couple of miles from the public high school where three of my kids have graduated from and the other six will at some point. I've been married to Sandi since 1981 and in addition to our five biological children we've adopted four children from China.

When I got the "entrepreneurial itch" and started my own practice I had few cases, a "no fee if no recovery" Yellow Pages ad and zero knowledge about how to efficiently market and build a law practice.

I quickly learned a few things:

1. Law is one of the most competitive businesses in which you could be engaged.
2. There are plenty of vultures out there trying to take your marketing dollar.
3. The legal ethical theorists want to help make your marketing to look just like everyone else's.
4. Most lawyer marketing is either so bland as to be worthless or so tasteless as to be harmful.

I was smart enough to understand that just copying what other lawyers were doing with their marketing would be a foolproof recipe for financial ruin. I started looking at what other successful entrepreneurs were doing to build solid, profitable businesses. I found that the most successful business owners were great at marketing their businesses. I also discovered that they didn't play in the "we are the best, just choose us, please oh please" random chance marketing game.

So, I began to change the way I marketed my practice. It was a little scary at first because there was no proven model for this type of marketing for lawyers. I tried to find it! So I went out and spent hundreds of hours and spent tens of thousands of dollars to learn, implement and refine this new way of marketing for lawyers.

I changed everything for my practice. From the message of the website right down to the language we use in speaking to new prospects.

It worked.

Today, over 29 years into a very successful law career, the practice thrives in large part because of a creative, interesting and compelling marketing program that not only puts my firm in front of other firms in my niche, but puts all of my marketing on autopilot so that I can focus my attention and creativity on turning good cases into great cases for my clients. I no longer worry about where the next case is coming from and in fact, the most pressing day-to-day problem now is a "capacity problem." I guess I could grow the practice with more people, but I kind of like it the way it is. Like I said above, I'm not about to bury myself in overhead if I don't have to.

So, why wouldn't I share this? Here's what was happening:

Lawyers who saw what I was doing would call to "pick my brain" or "take me to lunch" in order to get me to show them what I was doing. I enjoyed that for a while. (It was all about my ego!) As my practice got busier and busier I learned that letting others drop by to "pick my brain" was a huge waste of my time. Most left and as far as I could tell they never changed anything. (Too much work, I guess.)

A few, however, asked for more. One day one of them suggested to me that I package up what I know and had shown them and offer it for sale to other lawyers. It would eliminate me having to spend hours on end explaining everything from A-Z, while at the same time permitting those who really want to invest in their marketing education to learn and prosper. This would be "win-win." I would make a little bit of money if they bought and they could improve their practice if they studied and implemented.

I certainly could not keep letting lawyers "pick my brain" for free, could I?

In October 2005 I made the "plunge," putting pencil to paper and designed Great Legal Marketing. Just four months later I offered my product to the marketplace by letting a few lawyers with whom I had corresponded over the years know what I was doing. I started small and was vastly underpriced. I began working with a small handful of lawyers and six months later we had our first in-person mastermind group meeting. There we were, eight of us around the table, sharing, for the first time, extraordinary marketing secrets that each of us use in our own geographic and practice niches.

I was off and running with Great Legal Marketing... but always in the context of a part-time business underneath a full-time law practice and a really full-time family life.

You might be asking why, if I'm so good at marketing, I'm not a "regular" on the seminar circuit. There are several reasons. First, I have no desire to travel extensively. Each time I am out of town it's almost guaranteed that I'm going to miss some of the kids' sporting events or a play or a "back to school night." My family is my highest priority.

Next, as I said before, I am a solo practitioner running a full time law practice. Yes, it helps tremendously to have lawyers from all over the country know who you are and refer you cases and help you track down experts, but the work still has to get done. I meet clients, take and defend depositions, handle mediations and try cases. I couldn't do that if I was showing up in a new city each week to do a seminar. I have no interest in working THAT HARD in my part time business.

With sold-out seminars each time I do them (including one done each year in Northern Virginia) there really is no reason for me to undertake the logistics necessary to travel around the country nor to put up with the hassle and indignity of air travel. Lawyers travel from across the United States and Canada to Northern Virginia -- what could be better for me than that? I also turn down virtually every invitation to speak to lawyers at the regular CLE type seminars. I've just found that most of the lawyers who attend a CLE marketing seminar aren't THAT serious about getting better—they are just "scratching their marketing itch."

Anyone who knows me or has seen me speak publicly knows that I am passionate about helping lawyers improve their practices and their public images so that they can live saner lives and be heroes to their families and clients. What little public speaking I do, I most definitely love. I have deliberately decided, however, to keep Great Legal Marketing simple and as small as possible. It is run on a part-time basis with several (very, very talented) part-time employees and virtual assistants. (One way I keep membership small is by not tolerating whiners. You whine and you are gone.) I love working with winners and I do tend to repel the losers.

Finally, one last (but really cool) reason why I teach marketing and run Great Legal Marketing:

I have hundreds of members of Great Legal Marketing who send me their best new marketing ideas and strategies, "compete" for mention in my newsletter and vie to be included in one of my elite mastermind groups. In other words, I have built a tollbooth through which some of the most innovative new ideas in lawyer marketing and advertising pass. I take the best of the best of those ideas and test them in my own practice, refine them if need be, and share them with the rest of the membership. How cool is that?

Finally, as you may guess, my part-time business not only makes my law practice more profitable (because I actually implement new ideas every day), but it is in and of itself enormously profitable. I am living the entrepreneurial life: I am maximizing my gifts and talents to provide something that the market believes is useful while maintaining a pretty balanced life. The lawyers who are members, including mastermind members who pay $18,000 per year to be in one of my groups, would not remain if they did not believe that they were getting tremendous value out of their association with me. After all, lawyers are highly skeptical, aren't they?

RESOURCES FOR SMART LAWYERS

www.GreatLegalMarketing.com- the place for lawyers who understand that a great business is the foundation for great service to family and clients.

www.GreatMarketingBooks.com-my own list of marketing books that really don't have anything to do with "legal marketing" per se (and that's exactly the point)

www.DanKennedyAndBenGlass.com-free trial subscription to the very best marketing newsletter for small business owners and entrepreneurs.

www.Ultimate-Success-Secret.com-my own book on success co-authored with Dan Kennedy.

www.FosterWebMarketing.com-a web designer who gets it.

www.McMannisDuplication.com-great vendor for getting your newsletter out the door.

www.GLM-Software.com—see my video about infusion soft a very powerful crm software for managing your marketing.

www.TopPractices.com-Rem Jackson, my personal mind set" coach and "guru" to helping professional practices grow.

www.RadioForLegal.com—Harmony Tenney an expert at helping lawyers craft a message for radio

www.GoDaddy.com -used to purchase multiple domain names for direct response advertising.

www.WordAssociationPublishers.com-become a respected authority as an author in 90 days.

www.YourROIguy.com-toll free recorded message lines to be used to track your marketing.

www.Speak-Write.com-digital dictation service to help move projects from your brain to paper very fast. It now has a cool IPhone app!

www.SendTheBrownies.com--on-line cards and management of your birthday/ anniversary/holiday card sending

www.MullinsMediaGroup.com Chris Mullins will teach your staff how to answer the phone so that your good marketing does not get "killed" by your receptionist.

www.CallRuby.com-a very good virtual receptionist system. Our phones are answered in Portland, Oregon and I'm in Virginia.

www.elance.com-need a marketing piece designed? Bid it out.

www.BenGlassSuccesssStore.com-some of the classics of "success" literature.

www.SubmitYourArticle.com-when you write any article submit it to one or more article submission sites.

www.PRweb.com -press release distribution site.

www.Odesk.com- a global service marketplace for small and medium sized business to hire, manage, and pay remote freelancers or teams.

> **Note**: yes, there are lots of other great resources and I am always looking for new recommendations to make. You can email me your suggestion (and tell me why they should be added to the list at ben@ benglasslaw.com)

WHO IS BEN GLASS

Benjamin W. Glass, III is a practicing personal injury and medical malpractice attorney in Fairfax, Virginia. Mr. Glass is the founder of Great Legal Marketing, which provides an effective marketing system designed specifically for attorneys.

Mr. Glass started his own solo practice in 1995, focusing on personal injury, medical malpractice and ERISA and private disability insurance law. Through his experience in testing various marketing techniques, he has discovered what truly works and has implemented his knowledge into the creation of Great Legal Marketing in 2005. Hundreds of lawyers in the United States and Canada have already joined Great Legal Marketing and are watching their practices explode.

Because of Mr. Glass's innovative approach to effective, ethical and outside the box marketing for lawyers, he has been recognized as America's premier authority on this subject. He has been featured in or quoted by *The Washington Post*, *Washing Post Magazine*, *Newsweek*, *USA Today*, ABC News Online, *Wall Street Journal* and "The Next Big Thing" Radio Show. Mr. Glass has been interviewed on television, including the stations, ABC, NBC, Fox and Cox, as well as the show, "Leading Experts TV."

Mr. Glass is a professional speaker and published author. His best selling consumer books include, *The Truth About Lawyer Advertising* (TheTruthAboutLawyerAds.com), *Five Deadly Sins That Can Wreck Your Accident Case* (TheAccidentBook.com), *Why Most Malpractice Victims Never Recover a Dime* (TheMalpracticeBook.com) and *Robbery Without a Gun* (RobberyWithoutaGun.com). He has also co-authored numerous books for entrepreneurs and business owners, including, *Shift Happens: America's Premier Experts Reveal Their Biggest Secrets to Help You Thrive in the New*

Economy, The Ultimate Success Secret (Ultimate-Success-Secret.com) and *Carry Your Own Leash: The Entrepreneur's Guide to Autonomy and Success* (CarryYourOwnLeash.com).

In addition to his books, Mr. Glass has also created the highly sought after audio CD's, *Success in America: What Every American Should Know About Leading a Life of Significance* (SuccessInAmericaNow.com) and *Militant Time Management for Attorneys* (MilitantTimeManagement.com).

Mr. Glass graduated from George Mason University School of Law in 1983. He is frequently invited to lecture in continuing legal education seminars on a variety of topics.

Follow Ben Glass on Facebook at Facebook.com/LiveLifeVeryBig and on Twitter at Twitter.com/BenGlass.

FREE CD WITH AD EXAMPLES, TV AND RADIO COMMERCIALS

Would you like to receive a free CD with color copies of the examples I use in this book? Get periodic updates about the latest in lawyer marketing? Be among the first to know when I discover a new vendor or service that can help you get things done faster? Do you want the latest information on "Ethics in Legal Advertising" Notice (and my commentary)?

All you have to do is register your copy of this book.

Do it today and I'll also email you a copy of my free special report: *Why The Billable Hour is a Really Bad Business Model*.

Go to www.RegisterTheBook.com

FREE VIDEO MESSAGE AT LOSERFREEZONE.COM

Since the members of Great Legal Marketing are playing in a "Loser Free Zone" I've got a video message for you at LoserFreeZone.com. You might want to look at it now if you are near a computer because in the video I reveal the top three excuses that lawyers make for not being successful.

BUY A SHARE OF THE FUTURE IN YOUR COMMUNITY

These certificates make great holiday, graduation and birthday gifts that can be personalized with the recipient's name. The cost of one S.H.A.R.E. or one square foot is $54.17. The personalized certificate is suitable for framing and will state the number of shares purchased and the amount of each share, as well as the recipient's name. The home that you participate in "building" will last for many years and will continue to grow in value.

Here is a sample SHARE certificate:

THIS CERTIFIES THAT
YOUR NAME HERE
HAS INVESTED IN A HOME FOR A DESERVING FAMILY

1985-2010
TWENTY-FIVE YEARS OF BUILDING FUTURES
IN OUR COMMUNITY ONE HOME AT A TIME

1200 SQUARE FOOT HOUSE @ $65,009 = $54.17 PER SQUARE FOOT
This certificate represents a tax deductible donation. It has no cash value.

YES, I WOULD LIKE TO HELP!

I support the work that Habitat for Humanity does and I want to be part of the excitement! As a donor, I will receive periodic updates on your construction activities but, more importantly, I know my gift will help a family in our community realize the dream of homeownership. **I would like to SHARE in your efforts against substandard housing in my community!** *(Please print below)*

PLEASE SEND ME _____ SHARES at $54.17 EACH = $ $_____

In Honor Of: _____

Occasion: (Circle One)   HOLIDAY   BIRTHDAY   ANNIVERSARY

    OTHER: _____

Address of Recipient: _____

Gift From: _____   *Donor Address:* _____

Donor Email: _____

I AM ENCLOSING A CHECK FOR $ $_____ PAYABLE TO HABITAT FOR HUMANITY <u>OR</u> PLEASE CHARGE MY VISA OR MASTERCARD *(CIRCLE ONE)*

Card Number _____   Expiration Date: _____

Name as it appears on Credit Card _____   Charge Amount $ _____

Signature _____

Billing Address _____

Telephone # Day _____   Eve _____

PLEASE NOTE: Your contribution is tax-deductible to the fullest extent allowed by law.
Habitat for Humanity • P.O. Box 1443 • Newport News, VA 23601 • 757-596-5553
www.HelpHabitatforHumanity.org